Lutheran Mzungu

My Encounter with Cultural Difference
Teaching in Tanzania

Dot Radius Kasik Ph.D.

ISBN 978-1-0980-2693-6 (paperback)
ISBN 978-1-0980-2694-3 (digital)

Christian Faith Publishing, Inc.
832 Park Avenue
Meadville, PA 16335
www.christianfaithpublishing.com

Printed in the United States of America

Introduction

Dear Rev. Dr. Richard Lubawa

Greetings! We are Russ Hilliard and Dot Kasik, and we are writing to introduce ourselves to you and to the community at Tumaini Lutheran University. We plan to be in Tanzania for the spring semester of 2009 and would like to teach at Tumaini during that time...

I sent my letter off to Vice Provost Lubawa electronically. Russ and I had been talking about spending a semester teaching at Tumaini in Iringa, Tanzania, for a couple of years. Originally, we'd dreamed that the four of us—Russ and I and our spouses—would go together, but practical life finally made that seem impossible. Russ and his wife Jo are both attorneys; Kurt is an accountant, and I an academic writing consultant. Russ and I would be able to manage some of our regular work via Internet, but at least half of us needed to stay in the States and work.

After a week with no reply, I resent. A month went by. No reply. What was wrong? Surely Tumaini would want us to come; they were getting two fairly competent professors for an entire semester for free. We knew of other professors who had secured temporary positions at Tumaini quite easily, and some had lesser credentials than ours. Of course, they would want us. Our good friend Joe had assured us they would.

Joe Lugalla had introduced us to the idea of teaching at Tumaini. He was head of the Department of Anthropology at the University of New Hampshire but a native of Tanzania. One of the first things he'd done after his move to the States was look for a Lutheran congregation. He joined ours, Holy Trinity, and asked if we'd be interested in forming a relationship with his home congregation in Isimani.

On the map, Isimani shows up as a cohesive dot, a small town, an hour's drive from the city of Iringa. In reality, it's a cluster of small settlements of farmers spread across a drought-plagued valley. The people of Isimani are generally desperately poor but eternally optimistic. A relationship with Americans would feed their hopes and inspire them. With minimal financial support, people in Isimani could expand their farming efforts, open small businesses, perhaps even send their kids to school.

Holy Trinity enthusiastically agreed to begin a sponsorship. Through the auspices of Bega Kwa Bega, the partnering organization between the dioceses of St. Paul in Minnesota and Iringa of Tanzania, we pledged money for scholarships and promised prayer support. Within a year, Holy Trinity organized and sent off a delegation of a dozen people to visit Isimani. We returned after that first trip with a little more understanding and a lot more energy.

The result of that first visit was that there were now twelve more Americans in New Hampshire who had fallen in love with Tanzania and, specifically, with Isimani. Our enthusiasm was catchy. We'd seen the destitution firsthand: Isimani's failed corn crops sentenced people to starvation. But we'd also seen the other side: the pure joy in knowing God, in trusting that their lives were in His hands, and in wanting—*needing*—to share that joy with the world. We twelve related their story, and Holy Trinity responded. Within a mere three months, we'd raised enough money to purchase two semitrailer loads of corn. Within six months, as American Christians were readying themselves for Christmas, we'd created an alternative gifts program for our congregation whereby people could purchase livestock and scholarships for Isimani in lieu of filling our own stockings. Week by week, my husband Kurt and I were busy working for Isimani, speaking to groups, collecting money, and spreading the word.

All the while, I would get weekly hints from Joe about going overseas to teach. Joe and I knew each other both from church and from UNH. I'd formed a friendship with his wife. One Sunday morning, we stood chatting over coffee after the service. "You should be sharing your good brain," he said, and he reached out and scratched my head for emphasis. Yes, I agreed, but how would I make that happen? "You just go there," he answered.

So now Russ and I were attempting just that. I'd met both Tumaini's provost and vice provost on our prior visit, so communication with them naturally fell to me. But they weren't answering. Finally we arranged to meet Joe at UNH one morning to see if he could tell us anything.

Russ and I sat at the diner across the street from Joe's office and waited. He'd agreed to meet us before classes. By the time he came, we'd already ordered. Joe ordered eggs and coffee, and we made small talk until finally he said, "Now, what is it that you need to know?"

I called attention to the fact that we'd had no communication from Tumaini, that we didn't even have a date for the beginning of the spring semester. It was already halfway through October, and we needed to purchase airline tickets, plan our work schedules, get shots and visas, and take care of a host of time-sensitive items.

"Ah-huh." Joe grinned. He ate some more eggs and pushed another slice of toast into his mouth and chewed. Then he reached into his breast pocket, pulled out a sheet of paper, and unfolded it. He laid it on the table so we could see. "Look here." We looked. It was the printout of an e-mail message, a full page of text all in Swahili but with one exception. Smack in the middle of the page was the term *spring semester* surrounded by quotation marks. "Eh? See? That is the problem. These Tanzanians, they don't know *spring*. No spring in Tanzania. Winter and summer, but no spring. And the academic year has two terms, not semesters."

I went home and wrote a new letter.

That rather minor cultural misunderstanding was the beginning of five months of challenge for me to find my way, by turns plodding and plowing, into a place and a people so unlike anything I'd ever known and yet so very like everything I'd ever known. A conundrum for sure, but mixing cultures is always a conundrum. These were folks who spoke English, but we didn't speak the same language (British-Tanzanian English versus American English). These were folks who worshiped the same God and loved their country and family, but we didn't always share the same religion or values. I began to see as I made my way through these five intense months that it would be a lifelong journey for me to understand my place in Tanzanian culture or to understand the nature and purpose of what American Lutherans call mission and what—if anything—I would do about it. One way or the other, it would change me.

Much of the tension surrounding my identity in Iringa and at Tumaini can be summed up in the Kiswahili word *mzungu*. Walking through the marketplace in Iringa, I would hear it shouted at me by children, often by a very young child who would point, shout, and duck out of sight behind an adult or around a corner. It refers to someone with white skin and can be either strictly playful or a bit insulting. Its Bantu origin—*zungu*—is the word for "spinning around on the same spot," and even now *musungusungu* is the Kiswahili term for a dizzy person. The Tanzanians used it as early as the eighteenth century as a term for Europeans, the "aimless wanderers." Apparently, these early explorers were adept at getting lost in Africa; hence, the appellation.

But it's not that simple. The uses of *mzungu* through the ages illustrate how a word becomes freighted with meaning, particularly when the word attempts to describe cultural difference. Through the years, it came to designate Western culture itself, especially cuisine and lifestyle. Even now in some regions, it's used to describe something particularly clever. In these cases, *mzungu* is instructive about the ways Europeans were differentiated from native Africans and perhaps how Africa revered, feared, and distrusted their motives.

And this is interesting: peel back another layer and you find the connotations "ghost" and "apparition." Ghosts are generally problematic. It would be convenient if they could simply be dismissed, but they tend to be persistent. While I might find it convenient, even expedient, to blend into Iringan society, in Tanzania, I am *mzungu*.

No matter how many times I visit, how long I stay, or how familiar I become, I remain *mzungu*—outsider.

Being *mzungu* is off-putting, but the position is not without its advantages. It also makes me distinctive among my Tanzanian colleagues and friends, and so I take on the term willingly, with a mixture of apprehension and exhilaration. As I return periodically to these beautiful people, as I attempt to understand my place in their culture, will I forever be an aimless wanderer? I certainly hope not. I would rather capitalize on my particularity. People who are singled out, who remain with one foot outside the circle, have a better vantage point for viewing the whole picture. My desire is to use that advantage to parse out the best use of *mzungu*-ness.

What follows on these pages is an attempt not to ignore but rather to explore *mzungu*-ness. I need to know best how to use "this good brain" and other riches afforded me simply because of where I was lucky enough to be born. I write from journals I kept and still keep when I'm there, and from memory, which always proves elusive. I have returned with the idea of fact-checking only to find that I've changed, that places and people change, that circumstances change, and that my opinions and reactions change. Catching Africa is like catching a wild animal, hidden and wily, beautiful and dangerous. Will I like it once, or *if,* it's caught? No doubt some parts. Other parts will repulse me and push me into more exploration.

The setting for these five months, Tumaini University-Iringa University College, is in Iringa. Dubbed "the Harvard of Tanzania," it's a small private college cofounded between the Evangelical Lutheran Church of Tanzania and the Evangelical Lutheran Church of America. Until recently, it operated under the umbrella of Tumaini University, a conglomerate of several Lutheran colleges scattered throughout the country. It has now dropped its affiliation with Tumaini, along with the relational part of the name, but the college in Iringa was still called Tumaini during the semester Russ and I taught.

Iringa is a small city at the top of the Southern Highlands. In a country with so many nomads and street dwellers, population figures are flexible, but there are roughly 150,000 people in Iringa. Two major highways—the east-west Dar es Salaam connector and the north-south road from Njombe to Dodoma and Arusha—converge in Iringa, so it's a bustling place year-round. Perched on the edge of the Udzungwa Mountains and overlooking the Great Ruaha River, its climate is really quite perfect. Moreover, as the agricultural center of the region, it's easy to find good food. There's an historical shopping area downtown. It's a city rich in history but poised on modernity. Who wouldn't want to spend time there?

The Evangelical Lutheran Church of America maintains a close relationship with the Iringa District. Seventy-three congregations in and around the Iringa Diocese are partnered with congregations in the States, and the partnerships are arranged by the St. Paul Synod in Minnesota. Bega Kwa Bega ("Shoulder to Shoulder"), formed in 1999, formalized the partnership between Minnesota and Tanzania. The organization is jointly managed by Americans and Tanzanians and acts as a brokering agency for all donated monies. It arranges individual and congregational visits, and it fosters close ties between Tumaini University and American colleges and universities.

For the five months that we lived in Iringa, Russ's and my world would revolve around and through these three sites. Iringa would be our home; we would live in one of its neighborhoods, deal with the local economy, and hire local people to staff our needs. Tumaini would be our workplace. Bega Kwa Bega would be our resource center and social heart. By varying degrees, I would be *mzungu* in all three.

1

On Trial

(A codicil. First things first. If you want to understand why I'm here and what I'm doing, go back and read the Introduction. If you don't care about either of those particulars, don't read the Introduction. If you already read the Introduction because you're an English major, read on.)

It is one month into my Tanzanian teaching experience. I am standing at the front of Tumaini University's Academic Hall before a mass of students. One hundred sixty first-year candidates in law watch me. No one is smiling. They are not exactly defiant but not yet friendly. This is Law 103/104, term two. At Tumaini and throughout Tanzania, the study of law is a three-year undergraduate course, which means that many of these unsmiling faces belong to eighteen- and nineteen-year-olds. So far this term, they have been nothing but respectful, but I definitely sense that I'm still on trial.

"Today we're going to review Latin legal terms so that you'll be prepared for your exam on Friday," I announce as I stand at the chapel end of Academic Hall. The hall is huge and multipurposed, not square, not quite round, multiple sides varying enough in length to defy geometric labels. Behind me is the podium with altar and twin lecterns. Every morning before classes begin, students fill rows and rows of backless benches for worship service here.

Above is a soaring ceiling of exposed rafters, and rows of clerestory windows stream the glaring sun. Wires and cords from audio-visual equipment snake along the floor and dangle overhead. The university groundskeeper girls worked here after worship to prepare the hall for classes, exchanging benches for student desks. Benches are piled high around the room's periphery, ready to be dragged out for overflow seating when needed. Like today.

On a normal Monday, only half as many students would be crowded into Academic Hall, but today, because of a scheduling glitch, the two sections of first year law—103/104—are crowded together. One hundred sixty students with desks for eighty. The same will happen on Friday, not because of today's glitch but because cramming them all into the same space requires only a single test proctor. Cheating, I suspect, will be easy, but at this moment, I don't care. They need to pass this exam, and if they're ever going to trust me—this *mzungu* professor with her strange Western ideas—they have to pass with flying colors.

Inside the hall now is silence, my students' and my own. They're waiting. It's my move. I cough to clear my throat. "So take out paper and pencils and I'll begin quizzing you…"

Someone from outside calls a greeting in Swahili, and the young woman seated directly in front of me turns, grimaces, and gives a dismissive gesture. Long outdoor hallways branch off in three directions from Academic Hall. Sets of double doors at sides and rear allow for access—lots of access. I have come to expect people using the Hall as a hall, even as I struggle to teach. Another professor might scurry across the stage behind me, en route to a classroom at the building's far end. Random students use it as a shortcut to the mailboxes and convenience store in the opposite direction. One day a goat wandered in during my lesson on sentence diagramming. African students love sentence diagramming; the goat was bored. He sniffed around a few ankles but left complaining when administered a sound student kick.

"As you know," I say, "the administration has scheduled the makeup of your Latin exam for Friday. Qualifying for second year law depends on passing this exam with a letter grade C or higher." Behind the scenes, I have been informed that they had *all* failed this particular examination from term one, not because they sat for the test but because *en masse*, 160 strong, they had refused to take it. In fact, they had walked out of term one in protest of what they thought were unfair teaching methods. The responsibility for teaching them what they'd missed had now been handed over to me, the visiting American professor of English literature and composition with no experience or knowledge of law whatsoever. I was decidedly unqualified, and I knew it.

These students confound me. I'm used to the American classroom with student conversation, a Socratic give and take, but these students are silent. It's not that they lack diligence or aren't paying attention. On the contrary, every word I speak is carefully recorded in their notebooks. But when I ask a question or invite a comment, I'm met with a quiet stare. I might interpret their reticence for respect or even fear toward me, but it feels like more. There's something in their demeanor that I'm missing. It's taciturnity, and it's off-putting for me.

One reason why I'm perplexed is that outside the classroom, they're very different. In fact, the moment I pronounce them dismissed, they erupt in noise and action. They push and shove to get at me, to get my attention. A mob forms, the more boisterous (usually male) ramming ahead. It's classroom combat, complete physical chaos. A dozen or more students are immediately in my face, demanding my ear. Everyone has an excuse:

"Professor, I need more time for the assignment because my sister is ill."

"Madam, my transportation last week was not reliable, and so I was absent."

"Professor Kasik, I could not procure the text to read your last assignment. Our library is sorely deficient in book supply."

They follow me in a wave as I walk toward my office, their petitions becoming more personal:

"Madam Professor, I was dropped from the roster because my fees were not properly recorded."

"Dr. Professor, I cannot pay. My family needs the money. Please intercede for me."

"Dear and good Dr. Doroth, the rain has not come for my family. They cannot pay my fees. My mother prays for me every day, but

God isn't hearing. She asks that you pray for us. And could you find you are able also to give me something toward my tuition?"

Now, perched precariously on the altar rail, eschewing the solid floor where I wouldn't be seen, I smile out over the sea of dark faces. Ninety minutes of this ominous silence, I think, before I can hope to retreat to my office. A hand goes up. I recognize it as the hand of the student representative.

The office of Student Rep is a new and mystifying concept for me. Each class has one person who serves as spokesman and facilitator. Complaints, announcements, or formal requests, either from me or from the administration, are directed to the student rep. He's also in charge of getting assignments to absent students, of working out the library-sharing schedule for textbooks (most students can't afford their own, and even if they can, procuring them is problematic), and of copying my handouts. How the student rep comes by the position I don't know. Law 103/104's student rep is aptly named Godsend.

"Yes, Godsend?"

He stands. "Madam Dr. Professor Kasik." (Usually I'm addressed simply as "Madam." This is going to be important.) "I think it would be good if you could now help us learn these terms so that we might all have good luck in our exam on Friday."

"Okay. Good. I agree," I say. I'm thinking fast on my feet. "So let's get into groups of four or five. You have the list of Latin terms. I have some extras here for people who don't have the list. Let's use our class time as study time and help each other memorize. I'll give you thirty minutes to see what you can do. After thirty minutes, I'll give you a prequiz so you can see where you still have work to do." One hundred sixty faces stare at me as if I'm an alien.

Again, Godsend stands. "Madam, that is a fine idea." He turns to the class, waves his hands, and speaks to them in Swahili. At first they remain silent. He barks out what sounds like a command; the class begins rearranging their seating into small groups; and studying commences.

In my bag on this day are twelve-dozen Tootsie Rolls and six-dozen packs of Sweet Tarts. My plan was to visit a local Lutheran orphanage after classes to deliver the candy. Suddenly I have a better idea. Back in the States, I once taught a grammar lesson with candy as reward for learning. Students usually think grammar is boring, so I had to devise something to engage them. I read a story aloud that was laden with error. Students were instructed to shout "Gotcha!" each time they spotted an error, and as reward, I pitched the spotter a piece of candy. The students went crazy. Suddenly, grammar was fun. I'd hit upon two things even grownup kids think are fun: competition and sugar. Maybe candy would loosen up Law 103/104.

Thirty minutes ended. I pulled the rolling blackboard center front and wrote:

ANIMUS POSSIDENDI

ARGUENDO

CAVEAT EMPTOR

EX DELICTO

JUS ACCRESCENDRI

WRITE THE DEFINITIONS OF THESE FIVE TERMS.

STAND WHEN YOU HAVE FINISHED.

Students began popping up around the room. In no time, almost all were standing. There was some muted conversation, but still, no one smiled. They were taking this as seriously as usual. "Great. You can sit again." I wrote the English definitions beside each term. "Now raise your hand if you got all five correct."

About a dozen hands went up. I reached into my bag, pulled out a handful, and lobbed Tootsie Rolls to the victors. There was nervous giggling. Some of the morsels were pocketed, some tentatively opened. Requests about sharing were made. A young man in front bit into one and grinned. "This is American, right? This is good stuff!"

"Okay, let's try again." I repeated the exercise with five new terms. This time, more hands went up. I lobbed Sweet Tarts. By now there was genuine laughter. I repeated the exercise. All fifty terms went up, five at a time, and there was time for some of the hardest to go up multiple times. We used up all ninety minutes. It was by far the most raucous class session on campus that morning, possibly the loudest all term. At one point, two permanent professors appeared at the door to see what the noise was about. After a few moments, they shuffled away with scowls, and I wondered if I were to be reported to the administration. A small crowd of outside students had gathered behind the railing at my back. I saw an errant Tootsie Roll thrown over my head and heard giggling, but by the time I turned to look, the catchers were running out the side door.

Class ended. There was the usual jostling for attention, and when the crowd cleared, Godsend stood in front of me. He was not smiling. I opened my mouth to begin an apology, but he held up his hand. "Madam Professor, I must tell you that your methods are unusual. They are methods of teaching which are actually unacceptable in our country. But we had much fun today. We can see that you have the heart of a teacher, and our hearts are willing to follow you."

I wanted to weep with gratitude. I wanted to grab Godsend and give him a hug. Neither of those actions would have been appropriate—and I was already on thin ice here—so I said a simple thank you and shook his hand. Then I gathered materials together to leave. Godsend was waiting for me at the door. "Madam Dr. Professor, the candy is very good."

Can I just crow a bit? Can I just say that on Friday Law 103/104 experienced an extraordinarily high rate of passage in their Latin examination, high enough that at least one of their past instructors hinted that these students, the same 160 students who'd staged a walkout months earlier, had cheated. I choose to believe otherwise.

Iringa University College of Tumaini, University of Dar es Salaam. Whew. Big name for a school with five hundred students. "Tumaini" works, for short. It was established in 1994 with cooperation between the Evangelical Lutheran Church of America (ELCA) and the Evangelical Lutheran Church of Tanzania (ELTC or DIRA in Swahili). The "of" in the name means that this particular college in this particular place belongs to the larger consortium, Tumaini, which includes separate institutions spread across the country. The "," is because all colleges and universities in Tanzania function under the auspices of the government, represented educationally by the University in Dar.

Tumaini is a pretty little campus with a collection of attractive adobe brick buildings and relaxed green grounds, located in Iringa at the top of Tanzania's Southern Highlands. I had come here to teach the spring semester—term two—(please see Introduction for discussion of "spring semesters," introductory letters, and cultural divides) with my dear friend Russ, husband of my dear friend Jo. The day we first arrived, Russ and I stood a moment in the Administration Building driveway, linked arms, and just looked. Immediately surrounding the quad where we stood was an adobe ring: the college library, Academic Hall, and Science Hall. Beyond, another ring with offices, classrooms, dining facility, stores, and post office. To the south was Iringatown, and in every other direction, the Udzungwa Mountains—huge, towering, sealing the valley inside.

Our journey to get here had begun with another driveway conversation. It was two years earlier. Jo and I had been out together for the day, and in our absence, our husbands had been scheming. We weren't even out of the car before Jo said, "Uh-oh. Look at those faces. I see conspiracy!"

Russ reached for Jo and pulled her out of the front seat. "It's decided," he announced. "The four of us are going to Tumaini to teach for a semester!"

It hadn't *quite* been decided. When, how, what, and who still had to be worked out, but his announcement and his enthusiasm definitely put us on a new track. It would take all of two years to affect our plans. Russ and Jo are both attorneys working for separate entities in separate States; in the end, it was decided it would be best if only one went to Tanzania to teach this first time. Russ had a daughter who had gone to Iringa to work at an orphanage—the same orphanage for whose kids I no longer had candy—after graduating college, and he was curious to see where she'd been. So Russ won the coin toss. My husband Kurt worked in business and finance; he felt one of us should stay stateside both to earn money and to play grandparent to our grandkids. The college I worked for at the University of New Hampshire agreed that so long as I maintained Internet connection with them, it wouldn't be a problem for me to be away. I won the coin toss.

We weren't left to arrange things without aid. Help came from three separate directions. First, there was the ELCA congregation where we are all members. Holy Trinity Lutheran in New Hampshire maintains a rich partnership with a rural Lutheran congregation near Iringa in a village named Isimani. Our relationship began with the promise from us to send $1,000 a year, pray regularly, and visit when we could. In turn, Isimani pledged to pray for Holy Trinity. Our pastor, Linn Opderbecke, flew over to visit and seal the deal. A year later, a dozen more Holy Trinity members made the journey. What those twelve people saw and experienced during their few days in Isimani created an explosion in enthusiasm that turned what had been a mostly financial enterprise into a caring and expansive relationship. We'd been sending secondary scholarship money. After our visit, scholarship interest suddenly doubled and tripled. We had seen firsthand that this community of mostly small farmers had been hard hit by annual drought, so we raised money for truckloads of corn. We sent money to repair their church buildings and parsonage. We bought sewing machines for the Isimani Sewing School for Girls. At Christmas, in lieu of meaningless personal stocking stuffers, families in our congregation purchased goats, ducks, and chickens, which were then parceled out to the poorest of the poor in Isimani. Now this same generous congregation turned wholehearted support to Russ and me for making the trip. They would send money and gifts through us, and toward the end of our semester, another dozen people would come to visit Isimani.

Our second source of aid was really our first: UNH Professor and Chair of Anthropology Joe Lugalla. Shortly after taking the position at UNH, just after becoming a member at Holy Trinity, he had walked into Pastor Linn's office and announced, "There is a place in Tanzania called Isimani, and they need great help. We should help them." The Lutheran congregation there, he explained, had been founded by his own father, Pastor Joseph P. Lugalla Sr. Some of Joe's family still lived there. He talked urgently now about poverty and HIV/AIDS, about people dying, and about how we might help. I had met Joe and seen him at work at UNH even before he suggested an Isimani partnership. Thoughts about my eventual teaching at a

Tanzanian university were already percolating. I wanted to see this place he talked about. I heard a lecture he gave about his beloved country where every month he lost someone he knew to AIDS. "People are dying every day, so many that the population can't keep up with them." From our earliest conversations together, Joe urged me to consider going over to teach. "The US is not the whole world," he'd say. "You have to understand what is happening around you and why." And so by the time Holy Trinity plunged into partnership, I knew I wanted to be part of it.

Third, to make our partnership work, we needed a connection. That connection is Bega Kwa Bega (Shoulder to Shoulder), an organization formed to connect the Lutheran church of the Iringa District to the States. The ELCA partners each synod with an overseas destination. Iringa Synod, Iringa District, is partnered with St. Paul, Minnesota. A problem, but not insurmountable. Holy Trinity in New Hampshire would simply become an honorary member of the St. Paul Synod in Minnesota.

And now we were in business.

Russ and I procured Tanzanian visas. We visited local travel clinics to get our shots and malaria meds. We bought plane tickets. We packed our bags. Our friends threw a going-away party and pledged to e-mail.

My great *mzungu* experience had begun.

2

⋅✦✦✦✦⋅

First Night

Back up a few weeks prior to classroom candy-throwing. It's mid-February 2009, and our plane has just landed in Dar es Salaam. Russ and I have spent a day and a half eating airline food, drooling through cat-naps, and suffering neck cramps. After our long triple flight—Boston to Amsterdam, Amsterdam to Nairobi, Nairobi to Dar—I had only a few practical needs on my list: a drink of water, a cash machine, a driver/interpreter, and a clean bed. We landed with the flight attendant's usual "Welcome to Dar es Salaam where the local time is 11:00 p.m., the local temperature 40 C." Forty degrees Celsius equals 104 Fahrenheit. One hundred four. And almost midnight. It had been 28 in Boston.

Julius Nyerere International Airport's air-conditioning accompanies us through customs and immigration, but a furnace blast greets us as we pull our bags out into the open air. A quick look around reveals no water or liquid to be had, not so much as a soda machine. A cash window beckons, and two of my hundred-dollar bills meet the change criteria. I would cheerfully have given half of it for a drink. At least there's an interpreter. The only person left in the parking lot stretches out a hand in greeting. "I'm Peter," he grins. "Welcome to Tanzania. It is very late, and you will be wanting your beds. Let's go!" He speaks impeccable English, but he has no water.

Each of the church denominations in Dar operates a center where travelers can seek out inexpensive lodging. Peter drives us to the city's Anglican Center where he thinks the university has made our reservation for the night. The Anglican Center is quite comfortable; I have been here overnight on an earlier occasion, in a spacious room with private bath, a hot shower, and AC. But tonight, no reservation. We drive across town to the Lutheran Center. It's now an hour past midnight; my stomach, my head, and my body are all screaming for bed. And water. A neon sign over the entrance signals GOOD CAFÉ. GREAT AC. Peter motions for me to follow. Inside we find a lone sleeping attendant at the front desk. Peter wakes him. Our reservations are confirmed. Across from the desk are double glass doors through which we can see the café. Of course, it's locked up tight, and our now surly "concierge" says only, "No. No water."

"Well, at least you will be safe here," Peter says as he brings our bags in from the van. "Rest for now, and I will see you at six."

Russ and I drag our bags and ourselves up two flights of stairs and unlock the doors to our neighboring rooms. What we find is dismal, miserable, and dirty. Outside was the sign that advertised AC; once inside we find it's broken. I would so much rather have been Anglican tonight.[1]

My room is six feet square, the single bed reaching end to end and the desk wedged in beside it at precisely the same width. A broken ceiling fan grins down at me. The small high window opposite the door brings in the howls of a cat fight and brawls from a neighboring bar, but no breeze. A quick cold shower in the tiny bathroom cools me for the moment, after which I pull a nightshirt over my wet body. Under the mosquito netting, sleep is impossible. I ooze with sweat; my legs and feet swell, my head throbs, and my stomach churns.

After an hour or so, I stand up on the mattress and bang on the useless AC unit. I find an electrical cord to the fan, unplug it and plug it back in. Miracle of miracles, the fan begins to turn slowly, not fast enough to cool anything, but loudly enough to dull the cat fight outside, and I fall into fitful sleep.

---

[1]   The present condition of the Dar es Salaam Lutheran Center is much improved.

Around three, I awaken in the brilliance of an idea: there is water in that café. I'll sneak in, break in if necessary. I pull on a T-shirt and jeans, let myself soundlessly out of the room, feel my way back to the stairs, and creep step by step toward the bottom, toward the tiny reception area that separates stairs from café. On the last step, I'm foiled. Dim light filters in from the street, and in it, I can just barely make out a sleeping form. A man lies in a heap across the bottom of the stairs, clutching a rifle to his chest. He hadn't been there two hours ago. Perhaps it's the desk attendant; the rifle might have been out of sight earlier. I suspect from the sound of his breathing that he hasn't sensed my presence, but there's no way I can get by his bulk. As quietly as I'd descended, I turn and creep back upward.

I awake again around five. Had I dreamed my night expedition? No, it was real. By this time, my thirst is so strong that I suffer it literally to my toes. I feel both shrunken and swollen. My lurching stomach forces me into the tiny bathroom where I heave dry heaves in front of a dirty toilet bowl, then collapse into a sweaty, tearful heap on equally dirty tiles. Salt and sleep deprivation sting my eyes. Coming to Africa has been a colossal mistake.

At six I drag my suitcases into the hallway and bump them down the stairs to be greeted again by Peter's grin. He holds two bottles of Coca-Cola, one for me, one for Russ. The Savior himself couldn't have been more beautiful, the wine of the Eucharist never so sweet. Being Lutheran is okay again.

I have told this story of our first night in Tanzania many times over, always in self-deprecation because I actually seriously considered turning around and going back home. I believe the only thing that kept me from doing so was that my fear of ridicule and failure was greater than my fear of dying from heat or malaria or dysentery or any of the diseases I'd been vaccinated against. Sweat, heat cramps, and thirst made the immediate dire and the gradual improbable, if not impossible.

It had been tearful in Boston. I'd been on the opposite side of those security gates so many times, watching a daughter or a grandchild, inching along beside the rope, holding hands till the last possible minute when he/she took off shoes and jacket and hoisted a backpack up onto the conveyor belt. They'd turn and wave and blow a kiss as they entered the X-ray machine. A moment later, the figure would emerge on the other side, collecting, redressing, blowing a last kiss before slipping out of sight. Last night, Russ and Jo and Kurt and I had eaten supper at the airport, shared a final drink in the lounge before joining the security line, and then it was the same drill: inch along, hold hands, wave, blow kisses. Kurt and Jo walked away, and Russ and I took off into our Tumaini University teaching adventure.

Never one to suffer self-doubt, I'd traveled by myself before to foreign countries, even to places where English was almost never spoken. I'd taken new jobs on occasion with neither training nor experience. My pattern when faced with challenge or a new opportunity—jump in and worry later. It was the way I'd chosen my undergraduate college major, the way I'd jumped into my first adult job, the way I'd made major purchases over the years. It was the way I'd gotten married, for God's sake, and that had worked out well. Kurt and I were about to celebrate our fortieth anniversary. I told myself I had good intuition. I'd leap first and deal with the consequences later. When faced with something new, I could usually playact the part until it felt comfortable.

But this time, this place, this situation felt different. I was headed into too many unknowns—no hotel reservation on my credit card, no arranged restaurant meals, no conference room schedule. This time I was off the grid until—*if*—I could arrange cell phone and Internet connection. The language barrier and the cultural divides were great. Besides, some pretty serious sleep deprivation made even easy decisions impossible.

Thirty-six hours earlier, I had thought I was prepared. I had spent several weeks packing my bags, making lists, considering what to take and what to do without. First, there were wardrobe issues. We were spanning seasons; how hot and how cold would it get? Would I need jacket, hat, and gloves? I had been told that Tanzanian university faculty dressed "professionally," so what did that mean? Were there dressy occasions? Were there times I'd need academic regalia? Should I take my jeans?

Clothing issues were just the beginning. I needed medications and pharmacy supplies for five months. I couldn't rely on having a neighborhood drugstore. Even something as silly as haircare posed problems: salons in Iringa might not know what to do with fine Nordic fuzz.

There were academic considerations. I'd done some Internet study about the differences between British and American English grammar and conventions. I'd studied up on British journalism and subscribed online to a Tanzanian daily news. Tumaini had so far been silent about what I'd be teaching, but they offered majors in journalism and tourism. It seemed likely I'd fit either. My master's work had been in nonfiction writing, my doctoral studies in composition theory. To round things out, I chatted with people in our tourism major back at UNH. Tumaini's department focused on promoting Tanzanian culture, and that sounded enough like writing that I thought I could handle it. I'd once worked in advertising. Surely I'd be okay. I kept telling myself that all the way to the airport.

But now, here I was, really, really, *really* tired; and everything looked bleak. I wasn't physically strong enough. I wasn't smart enough. I couldn't speak the language. No, definitely, I wasn't going to survive. I would die in Africa. I would get lost, and then I'd be murdered. My luggage would be stolen. They'd cut off my clothes and throw my body aside. It would never be found. Kurt would never know what happened to me. My story would remain forever lost. These were my thoughts as Peter loaded us into the van and inched into the Dar es Salaam traffic to begin our eight-hour drive to Iringa.

The van was large. Even with luggage, Russ and I each had our own full bench. My first intension was to sack out and sleep. No way. Dar es Salaam assaults every physical sense. Our first hour was the inner circle where, even early morning, streets and sidewalks are packed. To the uninitiated, it's a boisterous mayhem. No one seems to know or care about traffic laws, if there are any. Police cars, vans, city buses, 32-wheeled lorries, sedans, and SUVs all jumble together. Bicyclers careen in, out, and through from every angle. Stop lights— and there are many—are ignored. Direction signs seem optional. And street vendors—mostly preteen boys—run alongside the vehicles to hawk their wares: flowers, roasted cashews, decorator pillows, newspapers, kitchen knives and spatulas, rosaries, and Jesus portraits. "Do not open windows!" Peter shouted. "Do not encourage!"

Now, almost 7:00 a.m., he inched our van through the tangle. We'd creep half a block and stop, crawl through ferocious but useless horn blowing and stop, then feel a jolt from behind as someone else failed to stop.

There was a bonus: we had plenty of time for people-watching. The entire population of Dar was on the road, and we had time to look inside each vehicle. Every make, shape, and size was packed floor to ceiling. A simple sedan easily carried a dozen people. Young men hung onto SUV running boards. A truck held a crowd; if the back was full, people perched precariously atop the load.

Even bicycles were loaded to the max. Huge baskets were strapped to handlebars and boxes on fenders; extra passengers, furniture, or working gear teetered dangerously. One ingenious cycler had welded extensions for a queen-size bed to his bike frame. There were bicycles loaded with concrete bricks and building supplies. Cyclers wove in and out of traffic and squeezed between lanes.

With his own window rolled down, by turns Peter chatted with and screamed at drivers and pedestrians, all in Swahili. At one point, we were blocked in on four sides, no significant movement as far as the eye could see in any direction. Peter leaned over and carried on a full conversation with a lorry driver beside him. The lorry began to inch backward, gently but unequivocally pushing the smaller vehicle behind it backward, its driver in turn backing into the next. The lorry motioned now for Peter, and our van turned sharply to inch past the lorry's front end, then off the road altogether and onto the sidewalk. We actually drove down the walkway, through street vendors and pedestrians, leaving road traffic behind till we hit an alley where we could avoid the main congestion.

As we drove further away from city central, vehicles thinned, and pedestrians took over. In Tanzania, only the lucky or the privileged ride; the commoner walks. Everywhere. Everyone has someplace to go and a burden to carry. We saw construction workers with stacks of lumber across their shoulders and road crews balancing bags of gravel and cement on their heads. Some were women; some appeared to be young children. A peddler had a metal-frame-like a cabinet strapped to his torso; it had panels that opened and closed to reveal pots and pans and various utensils, and it probably weighed a hundred pounds. Younger girls carried jars of water, canteens of cooking oil, and metal cans of kerosene on heads with more bundles in arms. An elderly woman toted four infants, one tied on her back, one on her front, and one in each arm. Peter, unfazed, maneuvered the van deftly around and through them. Obviously, he'd done this many times. We watched with our mouths hanging open. At one point, Russ remarked, "Africa is on the move!" Indeed.

It was hard to tell where Dar es Salaam stopped and countryside began, but by midmorning, we'd left most of the really heavy traffic behind. Now other obstacles appeared. Herds of goats and cattle, packs of dogs, teams of donkeys, and flocks of chickens—the road in front was rarely clear. Much of the livestock was tended by small children who looked to be seven or eight or maybe even younger. Most had even smaller children—toddlers—in tow. More than once we saw a really tiny child, an infant, sitting off in the weeds alone, no visible older person in sight.

To drive or ride in Africa requires that Americans suspend much of what we've learned over the years about safety. It takes both daring and skill. Travel guides will warn you about the dangers. There are many things to be careful about or to avoid—mosquitoes, snakes, the water—but more foreigners die in traffic accidents than all other dangers combined.

Besides vehicular traffic and pedestrians, other hazards complicate matters. Potholes are the size of graves. Portions of the road washed out by rain are never repaired. Gullies flow across without bridges. Vehicles are abandoned after accidents or breakdowns. Tanzania has no AAA and few tow trucks. If your 16-wheeler goes off the road, it often stays there until enough men can be recruited to manually lift it back into place.

Both Russ and I had visited AAA back in the States and procured international drivers' licenses. In this as in other matters, we thought we were prepared. Now, as we watched Peter negotiating the obstacle course that was the Tanzanian roadway system, we both doubted we'd ever be competent. He was as skilled a driver as we'd ever seen, certainly someone to rival the Unzers, Gordons, and Patricks of our Western world.

Up ahead was what looked like a village, a small cluster of shops in a clearing among the cornfields. Each boasted a hand-lettered business sign and front counter. One was obviously a service station; a lone gas—petrol—pump stood out front. Peter eased the van off the highway and onto the station's parking space. Immediately half a dozen young boys appeared at our windows. From where had they materialized?

"Stay inside," Peter told us pointedly. He opened his door and climbed out among them. First there was some haggling, then ferocious backslapping and handshaking and riotous laughter, and he climbed back in with his purchases. He handed the goods to us: roasted cashews, a stalk of miniature bananas, and Coca-Colas. "Breakfast!" he grinned. "First you eat, then you sleep. You see, I take care of you!"

We ate. We drank. And then we stretched out and slept the sleep of deep, pleasant, rocking somnolence—a healing sleep that makes the world safe again upon waking, that restores confidence and self-reliance. It's the kind of sleep that comes only when you've been awake for two days, traveled twelve thousand miles, suffered through body cramps and debilitating thirst, died half a dozen deaths from fear, and now finally understand that wherever you're ending up, there will be a Peter to take care of you.

3

Elephant Story

Iringa is an eight-hour drive from Dar es Salaam, provided you go
straight through, which people hardly ever do because the scenery is
unparalleled, and both Morogoro and Tan Swiss are located along
the road. This is the A7, the major east-west artery across Tanzania,
but that's not to say the drive is smooth. A7 is mostly two lanes—one
each way—and the main trucking route. Mostly it's too busy for
passing, so once you get behind a lorry, you're stuck.

Admittedly, I was mostly asleep between Dar and Morogoro,
roughly the halfway point. I remembered from earlier trips (after
nights spent in places other than the Lutheran Center) that the traffic continues frenetically as the road passes through a series of rural
villages, each with vendors out to grab your attention the moment
your vehicle slows. It's heavily populated until Morogoro, a largely
industrial community with the loveliest, widest traffic circle in all of
Tanzania. Its green swath with an inner riot of floral color is such a
treat for the eyes after miles and miles of brown earth. The city is
known as a fabric dying center; its name is printed along the salvages
of almost all authentic Tanzanian fabric. It also boasts some nice
hotels and restaurants. After Peter's substantial breakfast, we weren't
interested in food yet, but by now a pit stop was definitely in order.

And as soon as Morogoro was left behind, the Mikumi National
Wildlife Preserve opened out in front of us. We knew we'd reached
it, first because the van's wheels rumbled as they encountered the

metal grating and second because we couldn't miss the warning signs: "Elephant X-ing. Do Not Stop. Do Not Exit Vehicle." The A7 runs directly through the preserve. We could see groups of elephants off in the distance, and I remembered times before when they'd impeded our progress. If an elephant wants to cross the road, it crosses. If it wants to lie down in the road, it lies down. They're in charge; people wait. I reflected now that on previous trip across Mikumi, I'd been on a bus with Joe and a dozen friends from our home congregation. Joe had directed us to stop at Tan Swiss.

Along this rather austere stretch of the A7 the Tan Swiss comes as a bit of a surprise. It's a welcoming tourist stop with restaurant and bar, meandering gardens and paths, and airy dining *bandas*. After lingering over lunch, our group was straggling back to the bus along with our driver. The bus's door was open. We were settling in when someone shouted, "Elephant!" No one had seen him earlier, but he must have been lurking nearby, waiting to make our acquaintance.

We held our collective breath and our driver whispered, "Keep very still."

Now the giant pachyderm nosed his way along the side of the bus until he reached the open door. There was no way he was getting in; he was much too large to fit. Except for his trunk. From our seats we watched him wave it around, exploring first the gear shift, then the steering wheel, then the driver's pants. After a few minutes, which seemed like a year, satisfied—or perhaps disappointed—our visitor backed away, turned, and disappeared into the brush.

Stunned, excited, exhilarated, thrilled, we couldn't believe our luck to be so near; we could have reached out and touched him! Conversation exploded; adrenalin flowed. Some of us regretted not having grabbed our cameras. No one had been frightened; it had happened too quickly. Our driver identified the elephant for us as male but a teenager, not quite mature.

An African bull elephant typically weighs in at 15,400 pounds. Even a young bull could have dispensed with our vehicle if he'd wanted to. It retrospect, it was lucky none of us knew how close we'd come to annihilation.

I told Peter and Russ my elephant story. Peter chuckled appreciatively, but I don't think Russ quite believed it. The elephants we caught sight of now were in the distance. There were, however, herds of zebras, giraffes, and elands racing alongside the road for their own entertainment. The Mikumi stretches 3,230 square kilometers, over great flat stretches of savannah, always with the majestic Rubeho Mountains looming in the distance. Peter's former job, we learned, prior to working for Bega Kwa Bega, was as a safari guide. He regaled us now across the great expanse with descriptions and facts about whichever exotic creature appeared. "Ah, there's a zebra harem!" he'd call out. "*Punda milia* in Swahili. Black with white stripes, not white with black. Did you know each one's stripes are unique?" And then a few minutes later, "Ah, elands. Look! See the females? They're paler in color. *Pofu.*" We sat on the edge of our seats, and our cameras came out. "No, do not bother. Too far away. You'll have a better photo chance later." Indeed, too far away—his trained eye saw animals in the distance that we never managed to spot.

Finally we trundled over another set of metal grates, left Mikumi, and began an assent up into the mountains. Now the road narrowed. I always have the sense at this point that I'm leaving one Africa behind and entering another. It seems here that the higher you climb, the narrower the lanes. There's no passing of vehicles, and you pray no one strays over the center line. It's hairpin after hairpin, sometimes hugging the mountain, sometimes on the edge. The scenery is breathtaking. Literally. Its spectacularity grows with the precipice. You can't *not* look down, and when you do, you can't *not* imagine your car losing traction and going over the edge (which happens daily, but—blessedly—you don't know that the first time you travel here). I heard the frequent gasp and intake of breath from Russ, and I'm sure he heard the same from me. Peter was silent. Until now he'd played tour guide, cheerfully narrating, embroidering everything with random facts, anecdotes, politics, and historical trivia. Now, however, all his attention went into his driving.

For a time we were at a standstill. Stranded between curves, we could see only four cars ahead of us, all halted, and behind us, a frozen row. Honking first, a few brave souls got out on foot to nose ahead. No one in our vehicle dared such. In twenty minutes or so, the vehicles ahead began inching forward, then gradually a little faster, and we were on our way, never to know what the holdup had been. It must not have been serious; had there been an accident or a serious mechanical problem requiring help, we would have been stuck much longer...several hours, even overnight. On earlier occasions, I'd seen how Tanzanians deal with roadside emergencies. If a lorry breaks down, for instance, the driver stops in the road, gets out, and searches for a tree branch, which he then lays across the road several feet behind his vehicle. A branch in the road in Tanzania always means someone is stalled or broken down up ahead.

I had a few breath-holding moments when I cast around for where to put my breakfast, should it decide to come back up. Then just when I thought it couldn't get any scarier, Peter zoomed out around to pass the car ahead of us. He cut in behind a bicycler—yes, a *bicycler*—holding on to the bumper of the lorry [semi] in front of us. We gasped. Peter shook his head. "He will die someday, and then he will be sorry." And he laughed at his own joke.

Higher up, near the top, we hit baboon territory. It wasn't gradual. One moment there was nothing to see, and around the next curve there were hundreds. Were we to stop now; they'd have utterly swarmed us. They plastered the mountainsides and dangled from branches overhead. They sat between the lanes, picking fleas, showing off fancy red rear ends, and *chee-ing* at the traffic.

"Baboons," said Peter, resuming his safari guide persona. "*Nyani.* Social and curious. See how they try to catch your eye. They want to show you their teeth and screech. No worries: it's friendly! Unless you open your window, and then they will be immediately inside. They will steal anything." These were gray, wiry, and skinny, with pointy black noses, fairly nondescript, except for those extravagant behinds.

Baboons and rocks—everywhere we looked was gray on gray. Occasionally a tree spiked out at a crazy angle. Our van nosed up, over asphalt, through granite, and I envisioned the road finally sending us end-over-end backward, down, into abyss. There were no guardrails. I prayed for our bicycler; he had a hand each on the bumper and his handlebars, and at one point, he lurched forward as if attempting to swap their positions. Thankfully, he abandoned the effort.

Finally the baboons thinned out, the terrain flattened out, and our bicycler drifted off to the side. The air felt thin, clear, and clean. Turning off the A7 at the Iringa sign, we climbed the final leg up the Ruaha River escarpment. This was our steepest terrain yet. From my first visits, I'd forgotten how terrifying this road is. I white-knuckled the back of Peter's seat and closed my eyes. Russ gasped audibly. Within a quarter mile, we'd scaled a New York skyscraper. A sheer drop to the river attended our left, a wall of granite our right. The foot path beside us—we could have touched the walkers—angled back and away from the road and climbed through the scree. It was crowded, bikes and people alike hurtling over stones.

When I felt the van level off again, I opened my eyes. We rounded a crowded intersection onto a broad street. Again the feeling: leaving one Africa and entering another. Behind us was the spectacular view of rock cliffs and the Little Ruaha. Ahead was African suburbia. Ragged little houses and garden plots, tiny shops and dirt paths, kraals and wooded patches all vied for visual attention. Everything everywhere was movement: children, men, women, donkeys, goats, dogs, chickens, ducks, birds, straggly cows—everything, it seemed, but fish. We had reached Iringatown.

Peter drove us directly to the Lutheran Centre, which is a guesthouse maintained by the church diocese in Iringa. We stepped down from the van to a row of outstretched hands. I recognized Don and Eunice Fultz who I'd first met back home in New Hampshire, then at Lindberg Terminal near their home in St. Paul, and again three years prior here in Tanzania. Don and Eunice serve as coordinators for the companion Lutheran synods of St. Paul and Iringa. Next were Bega Kwa Bega's Gary and Carol Langness, Trish and Roger Bloomquist, and Sally Harris. I would soon come to see Pastor Gary as a link with the Iringa Diocese and Carol as a financial guru. Roger worked out of the Agricultural Office at Tumaini, and Trish served with the Tumaini registrar. Sally I'd met over the phone; we'd had a long conversation in January when she'd briefed me on recent educational and political events at Tumaini and advised me on how to prepare for teaching.

After issuing an invitation for supper, we were handed back over to Peter for the ride to our quarters. As Joe had hoped and predicted, Wilolesi would in fact be our home. It was a mile or so away, down Uhuru Road (Iringa's mainstreet) and then up the hill, winding through an obstacle course of ruts and ridges, past an intriguing resort hotel, and finally to a small enclosed compound. Our house stood behind the stonewall. Peter honked at the iron gates, and a man emerged from a tiny shed to open up. "This is Gwamaka, your night guard from Tumaini, and that is the guard house where he will sleep." As Peter introduced us, Gwamaka straightened to full height, buttoned his coat, and gave us a jaunty salute. Then he grinned, bowed deeply while executing a two-handed wave, stylistically covering every welcoming protocol.

The driveway curved around to the rear and ended at what looked to have once been a patio but was now stone patches, sand, and dried weeds. Under a buzzing neon light at the back door stood a somber figure, carefully dressed in suit and tie. Peter introduced Lotte Chuma. Lotte is Tumaini's procurement officer. He was the man directly responsible for finding us lodging and would be our go-to person for physical needs, anything pertaining to housing or transportation.

"I now welcome you to Wilolesi, your home," Lotte announced and held up a circle of keys. "I will demonstrate if you will follow." He undid the back door's locks one, two, three, with explanations of the intricacy of each—"sensitive, very sensitive, must be executed in this order, pulling just so here and here"—and ushered us into the dark house. "The keys are for the rear door. You must keep the front door locked at all times. Let me get the lights." From the outside neon, we could just make out that the room was a kitchen. Lotte flipped a switch near a bare bulb, then flipped it again, but no light emitted. "Ah, yes. This light needs repair. I will get someone out here to fix it immediately. Just come this way."

("Immediately," we would come to learn, is an African term that often means "never." To Lotte's credit, a repairman appeared within two weeks and made "an evaluation of the problem." Two weeks later "a specialist" visited for an assessment. Parts were ordered then reordered as the first were wrong. There were several more visits from various professionals. As long as we lived in the house, the light remained broken. In Tanzania daylight disappears promptly at 6:00 p.m., which meant that evening food preparation had to be done in the dark. Russ and I developed a cooking partnership—I chopped, mixed, stirred, and fried while he held a flashlight. It was a good excuse to eat out most nights.)

We followed Lotte into the next room, and here he located a light. He led us then room to room, explaining the usage of each, pointing out steps, windows, door locks, selected furnishings, keeping up a nonstop patter worthy of any realtor. "You will enjoy this home, and you will find everything necessary to make your stay comfortable. Now here is a guest bedroom. Here a second guest bedroom. Here a bathroom. And here is the master bedroom with *en suite* bath," as he directed Peter to deposit our luggage.

Russ and I locked eyes. He opened his mouth as if to say something, but I cut him off. "Oh, no, you misunderstand. Russ and I aren't married. We're only friends," I blurted, "and colleagues. Traveling together. We left our spouses back home." I was babbling.

There was a moment of uncomfortable silence as Lotte stepped back to reevaluate. "No problem then. That is your business," he said and continued on seamlessly with his spiel. I caught Russ's eye again, and we both stifled giggles.

"Now come back outside and I will acquaint you with the rest." He led us back through the dark kitchen and outside to make a circle of the property. "You saw the guard at the guardhouse. Night guards will be provided by the university from 6:00 a.m. to 6:00 p.m. You will need to hire a day guard. We have chosen someone for the position. We will send him to you tomorrow morning and you may interview him. If he is satisfactory, hire him. His name is Cosmos. His salary is your responsibility, and you may negotiate it with him. The position includes gardening as well as guarding, so you will pay him accordingly. Perhaps I would suggest 70,000 T-shillings a month, if you can afford that. Six days a week. Sunday will be handled by a Tumaini guard."

At the going rate, 70,000 Tanzanian shillings came to approximately $50 American per month. I did some quick calculating in my head. Twelve hours times five days times four weeks a month at a little less than 20 cents an hour. We could afford that.

"I will leave you to get acquainted with Wilolesi, your home."

Minnesota Bega Kwa Bega folks dub the neighborhood called Wilolesi the "Edina of Iringa." Originally built as a European enclave and separated from Iringatown by its mountain location, Wilolesi used to be exclusively white. It's a mixed neighborhood now. Several professors live in the area, and Tumaini University owns one of the larger houses. That's where we found ourselves. "Maybe they'll put you at Wilolesi," Joe had said when we were in the planning stages for our big educational adventure. And again from Joe once we'd arrived: "Ah, you're at Wilolesi. Good." I suspect he'd had a hand in it, no doubt making discreet phone calls to Lotte and the provost. He knew that Wilolesi would be a bit of privacy; maybe not paradise but close and a safe haven.

The area is carved into the Igumbilo foothills of Udzungwa Mountain along the northern edge of the city. Leaving Uhuru Road, what was now our house sits on the third tier overlooking the city. Several gated NGO (nongovernmental organizations) properties are scattered throughout the neighborhood, giving it an Embassy Row appearance. Each sits back from the road with its view partially blocked by an ubiquitous wall of rock and iron. This is high-rent property for Iringa. Wingrid the Lutheran grocery magnate, someone we will come to know well over the next months, has a mansion on one side of our house, and the Hilltop Resort is on the other. Wilolesi has the best city and private schools, both primary and secondary, and the only noticeable commercial enterprises are a coffee shop, a school supply store, and the Hilltop.

However similar to Edina or comparable American communities, Wilolesi is purely African. For starters, every lot—without exception—is protected by some form of fencing. Wealthier homes boast rock and concrete walls with iron gates and guard houses. These are elaborately landscaped with hedges, spilling greenery, and floral cascades. Lesser properties are encircled by corrugated metal sheeting, wooden planks, or plain plywood sheeting. From behind most walls, one hears roosters crowing, cows lowing, goats bleating, and donkeys braying. Dozens of scrawny cats keep vermin at bay, and abundant brown dogs—the only breed of hound I ever saw in Iringa—patrol their chattel. Even in this wealthy neighborhood, livestock is as common as human beings.

Russ and I soon learned that our Wilolesi house was originally part of the adjacent Hilltop resort. Frequently featured in travel guides, the Hilltop complex was built by a Danish family as a resort and training center. In its early days, our specific house accommodated the complex's manager and then the aging widow of the family, even after it was subdivided away from the rest of the facility by a security wall. We could see over and through the wall from our defunct patio, and a lemon tree planted on the Hilltop side deposited ripe fruit in our yard. So close were the Hilltop guestrooms that we could, in fact, listen in on trysts and *tete a tetes* while trying not to hear arguments and drunken brawls. The house was obviously once a *grande dame*, dressed suitably with elegant surrounding gardens, paths, and seating areas. Allowed to be in disrepair for several years—rented out to a series of university transients who didn't know how to keep it up, didn't care, or didn't have the means—it was now a scruffy *dame*, but one that would serve us well for the next five months.

One last detail remained before we were officially settled for the months ahead, and that detail showed up at our back door the following morning, exactly as Lotte had said. Cosmos announced his presence at 7:00 a.m., not by knocking but by shouting from outside, "Hellow, American professors!" I was up and had even enjoyed my hot water *en suite* shower experience, but I hadn't ventured from the bedroom yet. I was still struggling with getting my mosquito nets back into their frames.

By the time I joined them, Russ and Cosmos stood in the backyard, deep into negotiation. The two were already shaking hands, having agreed on salary. "I will be very proficient as your guard, Father. You will be safe with me around. You will see also that I am an excellent gardener."

Russ introduced me as Professor Kasik. Cosmos held out his hand. "Ah, Mama, I am happy to meet you. As I already told Father, I will serve well."

"Call me Dot, Cosmos," I answered. "Come inside, and I'll make you a cup of tea."

Cosmos declined. "No, no, Mama. You and I and Father will speak here in the yard." Russ and I turned to go back inside, but Cosmos wasn't finished with us. "There is one more thing, Father. You see, there is much serious work to be done here," he said as he gestured around himself in an arc. Now in the light of morning, we could see what had escaped us last night. Surrounding us in a full circle from where we stood was nothing but brambles and death. Dead stalks, bare branches, and clumps of dried scrub littered the space. The only green anywhere was some struggling thistleweed entwining itself through dead underbrush. Against an old shed was a pile of crockery, much of it broken. More pots were scattered throughout the landscape. Cosmos continued his gesturing, silently pointing out one broken feature after the next.

Everywhere we looked was brown. Even so, the shape of once beautiful grounds could be imagined. Once upon a time, the yard had been tiered off here and there with stone fences, reminiscent of the New England we'd come from. Now crumbling, their fallen chunks were strewn through what had been lawn and gardens. I thought of the backbreaking work restoration would entail, the measuring and hefting to fit boulders and fragments back together. At home we'd probably hire professionals; the local gardening center would send out a team of young men with strong backs.

We followed as Cosmos led around to the front yard, beneath fruit trees badly in need of pruning, ringed with dead vines. Two straggly poinsettia trees struggled to bloom. Tracking the stonewall enclosure and coming around again to the driveway, we stumbled over deep ruts.

Finally Cosmos stopped in front of a broad slope of land, mostly bare earth, at the farthest corner of the property. Fitted up against the wall, the plot to which he pointed had full sun. "Here I would like to restore the vegetable gardens," he announced. "I will plant beans and corn and wait for them to grow. It will take almost all the time you live here. But the food will feed many mouths. While we wait for the food, I will work on the rest."

He led us back to where our tour had begun. "You see how much work I have to make everything good again. I need tools. So now I request that you purchase a shovel, a hoe, and a rake." Under the overhang of the Hilltop's lemon tree stood a ramshackle shed that had once housed chickens but that Cosmos would use for gear. "Not from my funds but from yours, and they will be left for the use of the house after I am finished and gone."

We shook hands again and agreed to go shopping this morning for the tools he needed. This man would take good care of us.

Wilolesi would take good care of us.

4

Getting Schooled

Having lived in Iringa less than a week, Russ and I had just attended our first Tumaini faculty meeting, and now we were climbing the flights of stairs leading to the Bega Kwa Bega apartment, ready to unload and unwind. The meeting had been perplexing, actually downright baffling. An evening with Don and Eunice Fultz and Gary and Carol Langness was exactly what we needed. At the top of the second flight, we clanked through their iron security gate and *hodi-hodi*-ed ourselves into the front room. I could smell tomato sauce simmering and knew a hearty helping of Grace's comfort food was on the way. Grace was the brilliant Tanzanian woman who cooked, did laundry, and kept life flowing smoothly for whomever was staying in the BKB apartments. Yes, these five folks would take good care of us.

Gary handed over merlot from the ubiquitous box and said, "Dot, Russ, we're glad that you've joined us here at Tumaini. Here's to a productive semester!" Russ rolled his eyes. It was nice to hear, but after this afternoon, I wasn't so sure I'd be able to provide the "product."

Neither Russ nor I had been expecting the meeting. Our days so far in Iringa had been full—learning our way around town, finding food shops and hardware stores, setting up Internet connection, and buying cell phones. Everything, we were finding, takes an extra measure of time and effort when you don't know the local systems. Setting up Internet, for instance, required three separate trips up the hill to Wilolesi from the service technician and several hoofings of our own to downtown hardware stores. One business, it seemed, specialized in extension cords, another in power strips, a third in batteries. There were trips to the local provider office to purchase minute cards, separate each for Internet and phone. We were off on one of these errands, in fact, when Lotte Chuma, Tumaini's procurement officer and our "handler," tracked us down. "You are informed," he said, "of the faculty meeting today. *Informed*, we soon learned, translated as *summoned*. Immediately Tomas, our Tumaini driver, showed up in a van to transport us, and we dutifully climbed aboard.

Once on campus, we were led to a large classroom in Administrative Hall. On the dais, the dean of the College of Law sat with his assistant. In the audience were five people: Russ, me, Sally Harris, a Tanzanian law professor (female), and an Indian professor (male), already fast asleep.

"We most heartily welcome and bless the two new professors from America for joining us today and in the coming months," announced the dean. Anyway, that's what we were led to believe were his words. Everything was mumbled into a pile of assorted papers on the desk in front of him. We would have heard nothing had the assistant at his side not repeated his words. They were definitely a dual act. The dean never looked at his audience, only his papers, which he persistently shuffled as if looking for evidence to prove a point. He'd say something, his assistant would whisper in his ear, we'd witness a private consultation between them, and the assistant would address us. It was amusing to watch.

"We will now be handing out teaching assignments," mumbled, discussed, repeated. "Professor Kasik will be teaching Law 103/104, Sections 1 and 2 each, with Professor Sally Harris, and Law 211."

That wasn't what I'd expected to hear. In my luggage I'd packed a carefully chosen textbook on international journalism and a composition text ordered from Great Britain through Amazon. On my computer was a series of (fabulous!) self-generated PowerPoint presentations on the intricacies of the English language. Obviously, Law hadn't been on my mind.

The items had been chosen with thought. In January, I'd had a long, informational phone call from Sally Harris. She identified herself as having several Tumaini semesters under her belt. Her professional time was divided between a college in Minnesota and Tumaini University. Her own composition textbook for Tanzanians was in the works, she told me, but she recommended a British book I should use until she was finished. I ordered it.

Law 103/104 was identified as legal communication skills. Okay, I could handle that. Law 211 was legal research. That one would be a stretch. Russ was assigned one course in insurance law. He was smiling. I raised my hand. "Dean, I'd like to request that Russ Hilliard and I be allowed to coteach legal research." My request was granted without consultation and before Russ could object. I shot him a glance. He looked surprised but nodded.

The dean and his assistant talked for an hour, mostly to each other. An occasional announcement was directed at the audience. Normally I would have been bored, but the panic rising within about how to bend my composition knowledge to British legal language and research had created a bit of a buzz just behind my eyes. I was relieved when after an hour, the dean pointed at us and gave a quiet announcement. "The visiting faculty will now have permission to leave while the department discusses private issues." We shuffled out with Sally, who gave us an abrupt goodbye and disappeared down the hall while we went off to find Tomas.

After we'd been delivered back to Wilolesi, I sat down with a paper the dean had handed me. "You will find this to your avail," his assistant had translated. It was a chart with TIMETABLE boldly lettered across the top. If I didn't know *what* I was teaching, at least I'd know *when*. But as I stared at the document, I was nonplussed.

Russ sat across from me with his own variation. We stared together.

I located L103/104A, L103/104B, and L211 in a stylistic variation of Chinese, top to bottom instead of left to right. Those had to be my courses, but as far as I could tell, they were arranged in a losing bingo game. Russ's L608 was the center square.

"Why don't I make tea?" I suggested. Perhaps a cup of Tanzanian tea would help us think like Tanzanians. We sipped and stared.

An hour passed before we unlocked the key: *block* meant *day*. Everything clicked into place. Again, we'd been thinking like Americans. We had assumed course sections would meet at the same time and in the same location, probably M-W-F or T-Th. Too easy. At Tumaini, courses and sections met randomly in various locations, at varied times, and on irregular days. So much for my knowing *when*.

Both the Langnesses and the Fultzes had been around the Tumaini block multiple times. I knew I could learn much from them about how to negotiate the next few months. Now, pleasantly whiffing Grace's tomato sauce, I sipped the wine and tried to relax. Surely they could help decipher things. Conversation began with Russ's and my description of the faculty meeting, to which the BKB crew roared with laughter. They knew well each of the people involved, knew the intricacies of their personalities. Not only could they picture the meeting itself, but they could recap much of the background preparation that had gone into it. Recent politics within the department had caused faculty upheaval. For starters, the dean we saw was acting in the interim after the prior's dismissal. Consequently, there was jockeying behind the scenes over the position with a bit of a power grab going on. Our acting dean had been appointed for the year, and he wasn't thrilled about it.

The evening was just the medicine I needed. Listening, I began to understand that my confusion was shared by most first-time American guest professors, and even that in time I'd catch on and feel more relaxed. The bottom line, Gary and Don both asserted, was that Tumaini meant what they said about appreciating our presence. They had great respect for Americans and American academe in general and particularly for individuals who came with Joe Lugalla's recommendation. They were glad we were here, and the entire faculty would work to make our time comfortable.

"So where were the rest of the university faculty?" I asked. Our Tumaini *Prospectus* listed seventeen professors in Law alone. There were over a hundred additional faculty listings, *sans* other international faculty, plus a host of part-timers and adjuncts. Forty-eight course descriptions in Law appeared in the prospectus, several boasting multiple sections. The university graduated 200-plus law students per year. Seven people had been in that room. Where was everyone?

I was full of questions. Gary, as I'd hoped, had the answer: "It's Africa." We laughed. "Seriously, there's no real explanation that fits our terms. It's their country. Their terms," he said, and then he delivered the line we'd hear time and again: "You can't make this stuff up."

Gary was warming to his topic. Obviously, he'd had to instruct other first-timers before us. "Don't anticipate," he warned. "Tumaini's a good school, and it's doing a good job. But it's new, less than twenty years old. Its administration is still inventing systems, and the systems have to accommodate culture. It's not like planting a new university in America where you have precedent to fall back on."

"Well, classes start next week," Russ observed. "I plan to assign their first project right away. Nothing too major, but something to get them into the library. It'll let me assess where they are in their studies, and it'll get them into the routine."

Gary shrugged and grinned. "Not necessarily."

Our TIMETABLES did indeed specify that classes would begin the following Monday. I'd taped mine up on the wall with sessions highlighted so I wouldn't miss one. The rooms where we'd be holding sessions had been scouted out. We'd been given class registration lists, and I'd stumbled through two hundred and five unfamiliar names, entered them into a computer program for grading purposes, and noted that over half of their surnames fell alphabetically between Mbeza and Mzumba. If I called roll, I would more than likely botch most of them.

The sign on the office Russ and I were assigned in the Law wing said "Guest Professor." So far, we'd met few of the Law faculty—they hadn't yet arrived, we were told. We'd made a friend of the dean's assistant, Renatus. He'd helped us procure two desks, two chairs, and a working computer, items that we wedged in between stacks of bound papers from former students. The Law school had been founded shortly after Tumaini itself, and no senior project had ever been thrown away. In a couple more years, after Tumaini had a

41

chance to graduate several hundred additional new attorneys, each granted their degrees by the writing of a dissertation, the guest professor wouldn't have an office.

Most importantly, we'd introduced ourselves to Happiness, the department secretary. As in academic departments everywhere, she would be our go-to person. Happiness kept the attendance rolls, procured audio-visual equipment, scheduled departmental meetings, ordered supplies, and guarded the copy machine. It behooved us to make friends. Easier said than done. Despite the name, Happiness was grim. She was the sourest, dourest person in the department. And she was stingy. I told Russ that first week that my goal was to make her smile. Russ told me his goal was to avoid her as much as possible. We worked hard all week on our separate goals, the result being that I managed to eke out twenty copies of my syllabus to hand out on day one, twenty in lieu of one hundred sixty because Happiness claimed the students could share. The copies were handed over on Friday without a smile.

Monday morning arrived. My first class was scheduled for 8:00 a.m. Russ wasn't scheduled to teach until Tuesday, so I arranged with Tomas to be picked up alone at 7:30. It should be noted that Tomas didn't speak English. We communicated with him through Lotte, and Tomas had proven very reliable. When he'd dropped us off on Friday, I'd shown him seven and a half fingers; and Tomas had nodded vigorously that he understood and said, "Seven thirty, okay yes," several times to reassure me. But at 7:30, no Tomas. At 7:45, still no Tomas. At 8:00 I phoned Lotte and explained the problem. I had begun to feel quite agitated, imagining a classroom of anxious, expectant students. Lotte, however, wasn't agitated; he was laughing as if this were the best joke ever. "No worries. Don't move. I will be right there," he said.

Minutes later, Lotte was still laughing as I climbed gratefully into his sedan.

"I don't understand," I stammered out, feeling a little presumptuous to have made Lotte come for me and a little defensive that I might be blamed for the inconvenience. "Tomas is usually so reliable."

"Here is the problem," he said. "As you know, Tomas speaks no English, only Swahili. In Swahili custom, the sun rises at zero o'clock, whereas you call it 6:00. Your 7:00 is his 1:00. He would have been here to pick you up this afternoon, right on time. He is very reliable, as you said!"

Lotte dropped me in the parking lot in front of Academic Hall, and I rushed in knowing I was now almost half an hour late. A classroom of students would be waiting for the American professor to show up. Already, they would have begun to distrust her.

The classroom was empty. The building was deserted. I walked back outside and noticed now that except for two groundskeeper women hacking at the front lawn with their scythes, the entire campus was all but deserted. I walked across to the administration building and found Lotte's office door open.

At first I didn't see him. The room was engulfed in audio-visual equipment, boxy desk computers, and electrical gear. I could barely see his desk. That too was piled high. Boxes were stacked precariously around piles of papers and files. I knocked timidly, not sure if he was there, and when his preoccupied "Yes?" came from behind the clutter, my inclination was to turn and run. The last thing he needed this morning was to deal with the needy American professor again.

"Um," I stammered a bit. "Lotte, there are no students. Do I have the wrong day? Where are the students?"

"Ah. Let me explain." He emerged from behind the desk and clasped my right hand with both of his. For the next quarter hour or so, we stood there, hands clasped, eyes on eyes, while he gently schooled me by example in several levels of Tanzanian etiquette.

"I welcome you to my office at any time. No matter how small the concern, my full attention is yours." *First things first. I had never been to Lotte's office before. I needed the welcoming permission to enter his territory.*

"How are you faring at Wilolesi? Is the house acceptable to your needs?" *This established our history, providing housing had been his last official activity with me.*

"Are you feeling well? What news do you hear from your family back home?" *Back in America, we offer the routine how-are-you, but we don't really expect an answer. In Tanzania, there's always a demonstration of caring.*

"Do you think it might be useful for you and Russ to have your own vehicle soon? Did you procure international drivers' licenses before you left home? I can make inquiries to the provost about your transportation matters." *An acknowledgement of another need and the offer of a possible solution always puts the other person in a receptive mood.*

"Again, all of Tumaini heartily welcomes you. We feel fortunate and blessed that you have chosen to share your knowledge with us." *Preliminary inquiries out of the way, the actual problem is introduced by transferring attention to circumstance. (And complimentary speech softens the hearer.)*

"Now, about the students. I have heard that in America, all the students faithfully report to class on the first day. It is not that way here in Tanzania. At Tumaini, many of the students come from far away, places where they have family and job responsibilities. The first day of class is the first day that their families or employers will allow them to leave, so you see that many students are still in transit. Then when they arrive, they have fees to settle and other arrangements to be made. You will see them soon in the line at the registrar's and bursar's offices. Some of them will need to arrange for lodging. Many things occupy their time."

He waited a moment for all his information to sink in. "I think you can expect to have a few of them in class next week. By the second week, most all of them will be present. That will be when we begin counting absences."

There is nothing like entering another culture to make you realize that many of your own practices are arbitrary, that just because you might be used to doing something a particular way doesn't make it suitable for another society. The whole concept of time, for instance, is arbitrary. When my watch reads 6:00 a.m., an equatorial Tanzanian looks at the horizon, sees the day begin, and calls it 0. An American university decides M-W-F class periods allow for the best learning quality, whereas a Tumaini scheduler realizes frontloading the week—M-T or even M-M—allows students to procure employment. However a country defines time, somewhere in the past, people found justification for determining it. As Gary said, Tumaini was figuring things out for itself. It had been cofounded by Americans and Tanzanians, but it couldn't rely on others' customs to properly serve the people it was designed for. This, I was to learn over the course of five months, was especially true of the Law department, training Tanzanian citizens to serve their own.

Gary was right. I would be learning many lessons, I would be learning them quickly, and in almost all of them, I would be vulnerable. I had to learn to laugh at myself and let myself be laughed at. Beyond the laughter, there would always be respect, partly because I was American and partly simply because Tanzanians are typically respectful people. My efforts would be honored, but when those efforts proved contrary to custom, I would have the greater responsibility to bend. I was in their territory.

5

I Want to Make Things Better,
but I Don't Want to Kill Myself

Again, I stand at the front of Academic Hall. I'm a full month into my Tumaini teaching, and I feel most days as if I'm hanging on by my fingernails. I'd thought lesson preparation would be my biggest challenge (American English prof teaching British Law…), but between Tumaini Library's legal journals (so many interesting Tanzanian court cases!) and Russ's patient advice, I have more than enough educational material. I have a fat syllabus. What stresses me out are the students themselves: specifically, their sheer numbers. Sure enough, just as Lotte had said, by the third full week of the term, all 240 students were in attendance.

This morning, I scan the faces across the front row alone, matching them to the names on the papers I've just collected: Violeth and Anytike, Owden and Abel, Blandina and Loveness, Godlisten and Michael, Rashid and Salimu, Fatna and Restuta. Again today I walked into class and found two students sharing each chair. On my lists from the registrar, the 160 enrolled in 103/104 are divided between two sections, but because of the walk-out during fall term—which gave them all "incompletes" on the grade roster—most are now attending *both* sections to make up for lost time. And not simply attending but turning in dual assignments as well, doubling my grading responsibilities.

A week ago, I'd turned to Sally for advice. "Limit each student to one daily writing assignment apiece," she said. "Tell them they have to choose their best to hand in." That proved easier said than done. Sorting out papers one night, for instance, I found a paper from Conseta Chale, a second from Chale Conseta, and a third bearing only Conseta Chale's student ID number. Two others belonged to George Al-Jabry and Al Jabry. I don't think they were trying to be devious. I think that (1) African naming culture is different—looser?—than what Americans expect and that (2) oftentimes my American English was tough to understand. Language barriers or culture barriers, either way, I'm the minority individual here, constantly *mzungu*.

I move to collect second row papers and look across to see Godsend helping me. I thank him. "*Karibu sana*, madam," he says. "We are all hoping for you." *Hoping* for me? For my success? That I won't fail? That I won't let them fail? They are eager. I hope I can deliver what they need from me. Like college students everywhere, these are the brightest and best of their generation.

By turns, they exhilarate or exhaust me, and usually both. At the end of this teaching day, I am physically spent. Russ and I leave Tumaini in the late afternoon, deposit our books and papers at the house, and head next door to the Hilltop.

The Hilltop is a lovely, tiered affair—its restaurant, banquet rooms, and hotel suites escalating up the hillside. Hence the name and the accompanying rating in travel sites. Its outdoor dining, *bandas* are the perfect place for relaxation, libation, and local color. Moments after we seat ourselves, Robert, the lone waiter, appears. Already we feel we know Robert well.

"Red wine, *one*!" as he points to me, and "cold Kili, *one*!" for Russ. Robert grins at his own cleverness. We laugh and nod, and he disappears to fetch our drinks.

We sip and watch the valley turn from brown to gold under a theatrical sky. Nowhere on earth can match the Udzungwa mountain's paroxysm of color. Sundown comes early in these elevations, 6:00 a.m. by a Western clock or 12:00 p.m. (*saa kumi na mbili jioni*) by the Tanzanian clock and within minutes of daily consistency so

nigh the equator. From the Hilltop, the valley stretches out in panoramic view. Iringa runs before us, north from Tumaini's edge to
the Roman Church property and the old Danish compound; then
to the Lutheran Cathedral, Central Market, and old German clock
tower; and finally to the south edge, where the land disappears over
the escarpment to the Little Ruaha River. Directly across from the
Hilltop, halfway up the range opposite, is Gangilonga Rock.

Gangilonga means "talking stone" in Hehe, the indigenous
Iringa tribe. Today Gangilonga is a touchpoint for Iringans and
wazungu alike; historically, it was Chief Mkwawa's place of med-
itation. Mkwawa (Mkwavinyika Munyigumba Mwamuyinga:
"Conqueror of Many Lands") is a local hero of truly epic proportions. Throughout the nineteenth century, as various European
countries claimed, colonized, and Christianized the African con-
tinent, Germany grabbed the area then known as Tanganyika and
entrenched themselves. They established businesses and imported
goods from the homeland, building a railroad to bring in the wares.
They developed farms and hired—coerced—the locals to work
them. European-style government buildings soon occupied center
Iringa. And they brought Christianity in the form of Lutheranism
to the "heathens." By 1891, they had established a defensive base
(*Iringa* means "fortress") to fight the Hehe, headquartered in nearby
Kalenga and led by Chief Mkwawa. In a surprise upset, in mid-Au-
gust of that same year, armed mostly with spears, Mkwawa's army
managed to kill the German high commissioner and defeat his men.
Germany, however, was not about to accept a Hehe victory. They
sent a new commissioner and attacked Kalenga itself. In the ensuing battle, Kalenga was taken. Mkwawa managed to escape, and he
spent the next seven years harassing the invaders. Sometimes mere
gadfly, other times downright brute, the wily Mkwawa never let the
Germans relax.

Finally in July of 1898, Mkwawa and his first-in-command
found themselves surrounded, and they took their own lives to avoid
capture. Mkwawa chose Gangilonga Rock as the site for this last act.

It's easy to imagine Mkwawa at Gangilonga in prayer. The Rock
is split perpendicular through its middle so that attaining the pinnacle

entails a crablike scaling between two lapideous halves. It's tricky but worth the effort because from the summit, you see the entire Iringa valley laid out in sacred panorama. Several old German structures in Iringa center are still visible today. Some of what you see now would have been in Mkwawa's field of vision as well. To him, the commotion in the valley must have felt like violence. But on the Rock, save for the wind, there is only silence. Any menace below is hidden underneath a mosaic of rooftops, each tiny red tile merging with the next. The air above is like incense where birds circle and whirl, avian thurifers wafting wind and harsh sun. From these heights, Mkwawa would have hovered godlike over the edges of his kingdom.

Making a pilgrimage to the Rock today is a popular tourist activity. The scenic hike includes paths that wind through heavy vegetation and rocky outcroppings, all great places for lurking dangers. Mambas, for instance, love to hide among rocks, and they're highly venomous. I know a man from Minnesota who wanted to be at the top for sunrise. He met a mamba along the way. Lucky for him, he'd taken along a local guide whose flashlight caught the snake's eyes before it struck. In less than a flash, the guide wound it skillfully around his staff, then flung it high and wide and far away up into the rocks. I wonder how many mambas had met the same fate from Mkwawa.

The day I made the trek, I was with a group of eight. We divided into two, making sure no women were alone. The first party of four had just made their way into a remote area when they were surprised by a couple of the local thugs known to wait around for vulnerable *mzungu* climbers. Their eyes are on wallets, anything likely to carry cash. Today they spotted a fanny pack. This was their moment. My own party of four couldn't see what was happening, the higher hidden from us by a towering rock extension, but we could hear plenty. The thugs grabbed, ready to run, but one of our guys stuck a leg out and tripped them both. We heard screams, then profanities in dual languages. We heard a punch thrown. More shouts from both sides, more scuffling, then two scared young men scrambled past us, diving into the brush below. Achieving the hallowed can be harrowing.

Sitting tonight at the Hilltop, gazing over at the Rock, I think of Mkwawa. Fierce, brave, and charismatic, he exasperated the Germans for a decade. Even after his death, they feared his potential power. They worried that his final act of sedition, his suicide, would become something sacred to the Hehe, so they removed the head from his corpse and sent it off to Germany. This, they reasoned, was his final defeat. But they miscalculated. German occupation wouldn't be the end of the story. The visionary Mkwawa probably drew comfort in knowing that the Hehe would never really acquiesce. His faith in them was well-placed. In the ensuing years, two of his direct descendants, a son and grandson, would get themselves elected as government officials, the second remaining in office long enough to see Tanganyika evolve into independent Tanzania. Even today, Mkwawa's legacy lives on. Many present-day leaders in government, business, and the Lutheran Church in and around the Iringa District claim him as ancestor.

Such are my thoughts looking across at Gangilonga.

I turn to the day's activity, to my teaching, and to the two hundred forty Tumaini students now embarking on law degrees, each wanting a due share of civic influence, respect, fiscal independence and—in short—a voice in their still-emerging government. Is it a stretch to imagine an unbroken link between them and the enigmatic personality who called Gangilonga Rock his "talking stone," a stone as clearly visible from Tumaini's campus as from the Hilltop.

My two hundred forty aren't, of course, all Hehe. Internationalism and globalism have changed Tanzania's makeup. From my altar rail perch in Academic Hall, I see faces as varied in color as imaginable, deep Mideast chocolate, soft India brown, dark Africa mahogany, and black Massai ink. Globalism notwithstanding, just living here means confronting the Mkwawa legacy. His ancient, mysterious personality fragrances the very air of Iringa, and living in the shadow of the Rock, one breathes it in.

I sip my red wine and think of individual students. One of my favorites, Given, comes to mind first. It's hard for me to tell Given's age, but judging by his life experience, I'm guessing fortyish. He's quiet and respectful of me, of the other students, and—above all—of knowledge. There's no pushing or shoving with Given. When I ask for discussion in class, he'll hold back, allowing the younger, brasher crowd their chance. After a while, I'll catch his eye, and he'll be gently smiling and nodding. Then, if invited, he'll deliver his opinion, softly, sagaciously, humbly but with precision. There is no bravado; he's done with the brashness of youth.

At home, Given has a wife and four children; two more sons are away at college. For twenty years, Given worked for Iringa's Water Department, and the Department is paying for his Tumaini education. They hadn't given him a choice in the matter; it was arranged with Tumaini, and he was sent. As a condition of tuition, he's expected to continue with the department as their legal advisor. That means he's a full-time student, full-time Water Department employee, and full-time family man, earning tuition for two children in secondary school and two sons in college. I don't know that Given is Hehe, but he might be. A century ago, he surely would have been a fierce warrior loyal to his tribe, willing to fight for it.

Given's buddy in class is Edgar. The two are about the same age, both family men and committed Christians, but Edgar has a completely different story. No one is picking up his tuition. He owns a little shop or *duka* near Kilimanjaro, and he scrimped and saved for many years for college money. This year his sister, wife, and daughters are keeping the business going so that he can study law. His end goal? Working for women's workplace rights. The sister he's left behind to work his *duka* is divorced and handicapped. He wants his daughters to have easier, better lives than the sister whose husband threw her out when a kerosene cooking fire left her scarred and disfigured. Outside of class or the library, you can find Edgar at the Cash 'n Carry building center where he stocks shelves and carries lumber. At night, he sleeps on a sofa rented from a cousin's family.

Often I see Given and Edgar holding hands, the Tanzanian carriage between friends, on their way from class to library where they sit side by side sharing the same volume, shaved brown heads nearly touching, quietly discussing the ideas in front of them. Both men know what they want. I can easily imagine both men fighting and even dying for freedom, respect, independence, and Tanzanian values.

Neither Given nor Edgar would show up at the Hilltop. They don't have time to track the American professor's private life. Beata, however, does. Also a first-year student, Beata doesn't look old enough for college. She's delicately pretty but immature; she looks twelve, not nineteen. Quiet in class but with work completed and handed in on time, she hadn't really been on my radar until the afternoon she appeared in my office in tears. There were men in the class, she claimed, who were making her life miserable, taunting her, stealing her completed assignments and claiming them for their own or forcing her to do their homework. "Please, madam, you must make them stop!" The mother in me melted. I held her for a while as she sobbed on my shoulder.

"Beata, can you tell me who they are?"

"Oh, no, madam. There are too many of them. I'm too frightened."

"Beata, I can't help if you can't give me definite information."

"No, Madam. It's only people in general." I tried pressing for more information, but she changed her story. "No, madam. There is actually no problem. I was mistaken for sure. I misinterpreted their motives. You must say nothing."

Was she being bullied? It was plausible. I'd heard rumors about male college students resenting the presence of female scholars. Here at Tumaini, where the male-female ratio is fifty-fifty, men and women students are equally qualified. But sexist thinking often prevails, despite the university's best efforts, and there have been cases of male students threatening their female counterparts. If Beata was being bullied, I wanted to do something about it. I resolved to first say something to the class in general, something about the importance of doing one's own research for the sake of personal learning. And then behind the scenes, I'd talk to Egidio, head of communication skills for legal faculty.

On a cold night a week ago at the Hilltop, Robert had helped us lower the bamboo screens to keep out the wind. He took our order and excused himself in the direction of the kitchen. Russ and I heard a rustling just outside our *banda*. The screen flapped and wagged, then shook as if someone were out there struggling. Three heads popped up from beneath. The one in the middle was Beata's.

52

"Madam," she panted. "I am so glad I found you. I have been looking tonight. You should come to my church. We are having a wonderful sale." Beata belonged to a charismatic Seventh-Day Adventist group. "It will be a very exciting time." Her cohorts had their arms wrapped around her, and they stood grinning and nodding.

"Yes, please come!"

"I'm sorry, Beata," I said. "Not tonight. Professor Russ and I have just ordered our food. But thanks for the invitation."

"But then perhaps you'll join us on the Sabbath!" She wouldn't take complete rejection. "I know you'll come sometime!"

"Well, perhaps," I said. I didn't think it was likely. In fact, only days later, she found me in the marketplace and repeated the invitation. I was at a Maasai *duka*, haggling over a group of wooden bowls. She put out her hand to stop me.

"No, no, Madam. Those are not good. You must instead come to the sale at our church." Another sale? Wasn't there one a few days ago? "We have the best bowls! Do not buy from these others." I found her motives slightly suspect. There is something about Beata that I can't understand, can't explain, but also can't ignore.

I am eager to get to know my students, and they, it seems, are equally keen to know me. While they might be reluctant to speak in class, they aren't shy afterward. Outside of class sessions, social boundaries are fluid. My Western sensibilities around personal space and ownership don't work. The moment I utter "class dismissed," the rules change. They swarm the classroom front, surrounding me with chatter—questions, demands, excuses, stories, many of the stories more personal than I care for, accounts of their love lives, and explicit descriptions of physical maladies. I make my way across campus amid a small crowd. Rarely do I have to carry my own books, my jacket, or my bag, and often someone will be clutching my arm. At my office door, they line up, waiting to be invited in. Or enter before invitation.

Again one afternoon, I looked up from my desk to see Beata. I stood to welcome her, and she fell at my feet, arms wrapped around my legs, and face buried in my knees. She was sobbing. "Madam Professor," she hiccupped, "you must help me immediately. My family needs money. My mother is ill, my father doesn't have a job, but we have to pay the hospital. Please, Madam, can you give me money? I need it today."

"Beata, I don't have money to give you. Even if I did, you know it would be against school policy."

The sobs stopped. She stood, brushed off her clothes, and grinned. "Okay then. See you tomorrow!" She grinned again and was gone. I noticed there were no tears to brush away. Beata, the gadfly, was tenacious if nothing else.

Students everywhere are mostly the same, wanting an education, needing an education, and knowing their performance is being judged not only by the educational community—fellow students, professors, deans, administrators—but also by whomever is financing their education. But once in a while (okay, maybe more often than we educators would like to admit), a student distinguishes himself as so desperate about grades that he succumbs to dishonesty.

Such are my wily Mbuli boys, identical twins, Michael Joseph Mbuli and Michael Emanuel Mbuli. They are bullies; they may indeed be Beata's tormentors. When they come to class, they are proud, loud, and braggadocio, disrespectful of me and their female classmates. Their attendance is spotty enough that when they first showed up in my office, I couldn't name them. That met with disdain. "We are identical twins!" How stupid could I be?

The reason for their visit was that I had assigned identical failing grades to their papers for the week prior. They were plagiarized word for word from the Internet and…identical. Now they were demanding to know the reason behind the Fs. I explained. "But, Madam. We are identical twins. We share everything." Now I was really stupid.

I run into plagiarism problems with international students in the States too. Different approaches to research can cause difficulty. American higher education prides itself on the development of critical thinking skills. Our aims in assigning a research project are that a student will collect pertinent data and facts from various sites and formats, compare and contrast the material, digest and internalize their discoveries, and come up with an end project that says something new. Reporting the information is the ultimate step, but even the final project (i.e., a written paper, a presentation, a mechanical invention) is subject to revision and tinkering. Not so in many international settings.

And then there's the sticky problem of cheating by copping or coopting another students' work. Here the dichotomy is often between independent learning and communal learning. Americans champion individualism, whereas other countries may champion conformity. What one calls cheating, another calls sharing.

Tumaini is completely aware of these tensions and is doing its best to bridge the gaps. Its prospectus very clearly spells out their stand against academic dishonesty in all forms, including both personal cheating and plagiarism and in aiding or abetting other students to similar acts. When the Mbulis "shared" their assignments, I handed the evidence to Egidio. He advised me to assign failing grades but to offer half credit for a second chance. When they'd repeated the offense this week, Egidio took the matter up the chain to the dean. By now there is little chance that either Mbuli can manage to pass the course, even if their final projects earn As. Two days ago, the Mbulis decided to take action. They penned and sent a written appeal to the Dean of Law to have "Dr. Kasik immediately removed from academic relevance due to her attempts to inculcate the campus with Western practice." A copy of that missive had arrived on my desk earlier today, but Ranatus, the dean's assistant, told me to ignore it.

Even now as I sit contemplatively sipping Hilltop's red wine, I see the window of doubt opening a crack; I think I already know what lies ahead. Skip to the final days of the term, when they do, in fact, turn in identical papers. Those final papers will be the fifth such set for them. The dean has declared them unqualified to sit for final exams, but they refuse to quit. As I'll remember later, the stickiness of the situation will occupy central place in Russ's and my discussions for the better part of a week, then require a full weekend's worth of red wine and cold Kili. I will finally come up with a brilliant solution: using the numerical scale for grading published in the *Prospectus*, I'll give their combined paper a D- or 40 percentage points. Then I'll inform them that since it is a shared paper, they will also share the grade, earning each Michael 20 points and a failed semester.

(Besides mulling them over at the Hilltop, Russ and I moaned and groaned about the Mbuli boys' situation with our Bega Kwa Bega friends, especially the Langnesses, both of whom had taught and worked at Tumaini in past years. Gary and Carol returned to the States before the final purloined paper was turned in, but I'd kept them apprised of events throughout. A full year later, with Carol back in Iringa and me in New Hampshire, I received an e-mail. She was in the Tumaini registrar's office. "Hi, Dot, I think I remember that you had two students claiming to be identical twins in your class and that you ended up having to fail them because of cheating. Weren't their names Mbuli? This year, we have two students claiming to be Joseph and Emmanuel Mbuli, their records showing one born in 1983, the other in 1993, making them twenty and thirty years old. If they're identical twins, their mother's was the longest pregnancy on record." I had to laugh out loud.)

I've heard of students who, after being disqualified from Tumaini because of grades, unpaid finances, or other such infractions, will simply change their names and reapply. In fact, the cultural inclination toward name-changing is part of my present difficulty in sorting out student papers. The Mbuli boys definitely up the ante. Was even Mkwawa this wily? I'm betting the Mbulis get themselves elected to political office one day.

A couple of weeks later, after staring across at Gangilonga night after night, Russ and I took ourselves out to Kalenga to investigate the Chief Mkwawa Memorial Museum. Its centerpiece is the celebrated skull, encased in a glass box and displayed on a stone pedestal. Germany lost Tanganyika to Great Britain in 1919, after the Great War, and the Treaty of Versailles stipulated that the skull be returned to its rightful home. However, it went "missing" and stayed that way until 1953 when Englishman Sir Edward Twining finally located it at the Bremen Museum in Germany. Mkwawa was in good company. Bremen had a collection of eighty-four East African skulls, but only one of them had a bullet hole. In 1954, Mkwawa's skull was returned and placed on display.

The museum collection effectively tells the story of the great chief, including suggestions on how his personality still shapes present-day politics. Local people honor his memory. He left quite a legacy. Among the artifacts are various nineteenth century Hehe weapons, household utensils, the stool Mkwawa used for tribal council, and a few German articles. Russ and I spent a pleasant hour looking around and chatting with the guide. We were the only visitors. Finally, having seen everything and having exhausted our guide's stories, we thanked him and slipped a tip into his tip box.

Outside the building is a small garden enclosed in a stonewall. A modest, undistinguished tree stands at its center. Russ and I took a quick look over our shoulders and headed for our car.

"Sir, Madam. I must give you a tour of the grounds." Our guide exploded from the building and grabbed Russ by the arm. I followed as Russ was dragged back to see some neat plantings, indigenous bushes and herbs that the Hehe would have used medicinally. Our guide gestured proudly toward the stonewall and explained that he'd helped in its construction.

"And now I will show you a most mysterious thing." He gestured toward the tree, ducked under a low branch, and stood by its trunk. "This is the holy tree of Mkwawa. You hear that bird? That is the work-hard bird, named so because he says his name: 'work hard, work hard.'" I listened. I did indeed hear a distinctive and repetitive bird song, but if it was saying "work hard," it must have been in Hehe or Swahili.

"Yes, the work-hard bird lives here," he continued. "They say that he chooses this tree because it is magical. How is it magical, you ask?" We hadn't. "Because twice a day, once at sunrise and again at sunset, the tree glows red. Every day of the year, rain or sun, hot or cold. They say it's because Mkwawa's spirit inhabits the tree. Mkwawa's very spirit! That's why the work-hard bird, that's why the red glow."

Russ and I held our laughter until safely in our car. We drove back to Iringa for supper, then stopped at the Hilltop to reprise the day's activity.

The next day, I asked my students how many had been to visit the museum. Not a single hand was raised. I asked how many knew Mkwawa's story and almost every hand went up. We talked a bit about the famous leader and the Rock, about the Germans and other occupying forces. I suggested the idea that there might be modern-day Mkwawas among us. They were enthusiastic, several of them making the bold claim that they themselves would have taken the same stand as the chief, even to the point of suicide.

"Time to write," I announced. I chalked the daily question on the blackboard: "What is a modern Mkwawa?" And asked them to respond. The room went silent, save for pens skittering across paper. I gave them ten minutes to write, directed them to underline their topic sentences, and asked volunteers to write their sentences on the board.

Modern Mkwawa fights the modern battle.
Modern Mkwawas are people who want to
protect and improve Tanzania.
Today we fight the system sometimes our own government.
We fight the best way we know but not with swords.
In Tanzania now the battle is government corruption.
Use words and ideas, not bullets.
A modern Mkwawa studies law if he wants to make things better.
Modern Mkwawa works hard.
I want to make things better, but I don't want to kill myself.

I collected their paragraphs as they filed out after dismissal. Through the usual pushing, shoving, and jostling for attention, I noticed class representative Godsend holding back. Because his job was to speak for his classmates, by turns bringing me collective excuses, clarifications about assignments, requests for extensions, or complaints that a particular assignment was too difficult, I steeled myself.

When the dust cleared, he was grinning. "Madam Professor. Many students want to know. Did you enjoy your red wine last night?"

6

A Day in Iringatown

It's our day off. We take a tour around our yard to view Cosmos's latest project: resurfacing our driveway. With polyethylene. Every morning for the last month, as he's bicycled through Iringa to reach our house, he's been collecting plastic shopping bags and empty soda bottles. Now he's filled the deepest of the ruts with bottle-stuffed bags, added a few small rocks, and covered over the whole thing with a thin layer of dirt. We nod encouragingly at a repair that'll last at least until the end of the week, two days away. Before we leave, he announces that he will be busy washing our car this morning. He washed it yesterday afternoon as well. The heavy rains we heard overnight washed it again, and it hasn't been driven in between. But again, we nod encouragingly. Already we've figured out that washing a car is as close as Cosmos will ever be to actually owning a car.

He lets us through the gate. We wave him our goodbyes, and we start our day in Iringa. First stop: Hasty Tasty Too (HHT) for French toast with "real" maple syrup, a chat with Shafeen, and a bit of local color.

As we trudge down the hill in the heat, we gingerly step around and through ruts that deepened with the previous night's rain. In this, the rainy season, every day adds to the muck. We chuckle about how much money the CAUTION SLIPPERY WHEN WET signs and yellow cones would cost if this were America. Iringa's main roads have open cement conduits to deal with the rainy season, but these clay side roads have nothing. The road *is* the conduit. It's one reason we've eschewed driving today. We learned the hard way about driving through wet clay; it had taken an hour yesterday to negotiate the half-mile uphill, zigzagging our way to find purchase ground.

Our second reason is that the drive is dicey even in dry conditions. Knowing the location and depth of each rut is crucial. One night, Russ hit a pothole hidden in shadow. The jolt knocked loose the undercarriage rack for the spare tire. We stopped, investigated, and jerry-rigged the rack back into place, then discovered the spare tire itself was missing. After a frantic search, calculating the angles it might have bounced from each downhill rut, fence, tree trunk, and rock, it was nowhere. Could it have made its way completely down the three blocks behind us? Doubtful, because our road made several sharp—and somewhat illogical—turns, snaking around the varied structures. That tire would have caromed like a billiard ball to make it to the bottom. Once there, it would have hit the always crowded Uhuru Road. A rolling tire with any velocity at all could take out a vehicle or two, causing a chain-reaction multicar pileup and easily maiming and/or killing a dozen people, probably six or seven innocent but drunken party-goers in one car trying to get themselves from one bar to another and unsuspectingly rear-ending a packed *dala-dala* with twenty or more students returning home from a day at the university and going off to visit their seventy-five-year-old grandfathers, or else Grandfather himself was in the car and was now dead, along with his deaf and crippled wife. (Not an exaggeration. At a bend in the road where twenty-two people were killed in one horrific crash, a speed bump has been added. The locals will turn their glance sideways, suppressing a grin, as they tell you the bump is formed from the bodies.)

It turned out there had never been a spare tire at all.

So this morning, we slide our way through the muddy ooze down the hill on foot. Hasty Tasty Too is a mile ahead. It's tiny, maybe fifteen feet wall-to-wall, sandwiched between an electronics store and an auction block. Wild vines outline the porch, obscuring the sign until you're directly on it, which means that it should be easy to miss. But everyone—literally *everyone*—knows it's here.

It's a Western favorite: every tourist knows HTT, every Peace Corps volunteer and every NGO. The roving street merchants keep an eye on who goes in and out, and they know which targets at which to pounce.

"Hello, Mama! You need baskets today?"

"Mama, I have pretty batiks. *Zuri sana!*"

"Here, let me show you. I give good deal."

"Just look! No pressure. If you like, you buy."

"If you don't like, if I don't have, I can get for you tomorrow."

"Good price, Mama. Mine are the best in Iringa, no mistake."

I notice they rarely approach Russ.

We laugh, shake our heads, and press our way through. "Later," I say, "maybe tomorrow."

"Mama needs to learn how to say no," says Russ.

HTT's proprietor, Shafeen, once told us that when the original burned down, Too replaced it. We bang through the screen door and slide into an already crowded booth. Here the diners pack together; food is a party, and it matters not whether you know the folks sharing your table. You can choose indoor or outdoor service, but inside is usually faster. Either way, the banter is quicker than the food.

One entire wall is covered with menu items, one half indecipherable, the other half no longer available. Your best bet is to order a standard: mendazi and chai or samosas and hot sauce or chicken and chips. Chapatti comes with everything. There's a glass display counter with fried pastries—you can special order a to-go lunch—and two Coca-Cola machines, both mostly empty. From a high shelf above, a television blasts BBC travel shows. Almost hidden and totally silent, Shafeen's mom sits behind the counter.

Shafeen is a caramel-skinned Arab with a bald head, a gentle voice, and a generous belly. He plays favorites to everyone, especially Westerners. He's Iringa's unofficial travel consultant, tour guide, and social director. His life's aim is to make you happy. On one early visit, I forgot my wallet and couldn't pay the bill. "No matter." He smiled. "I know you'll make it right next time." I went immediately to the ATM at the bank down the street and returned with cash.

"How did you know to trust me?" I asked.

"I didn't," he said, "but the universe does!" He gestured toward a portrait high on the wall. From just below the water-stained ceiling, the Aga Khan smiles down over diners with enigmatic benevolence.

This morning, breakfast accomplished, we head through Uhuru Park, past the newspaper kiosks and the Maasai *dukas* into the center of Iringatown. Our target is Central Market, one of the two oldest open-air marketplaces left in Tanzania (the other is in Zanzibar). I have my shopping basket on my arm, and I'm planning to fill it. The Market, a cooperative of Iringa Valley's farmers, will have pyramids of color—carrots, beets, pineapples, melons, apples, lettuce, beans; you name it, it'll be there alongside stuff you've never seen, everything brought this morning from the *shambas* of Tanzania's most prolific agricultural areas. Along one side is a wall made from one-hundred-pound bags of rice; huge baskets of dried beans frame another section. Each tiny rented stall is piled high with the grower's best. Customers swarm the paths between.

I love being here. It's fresh and frenetic, fecund and piquant, all at once. I'm sated: wrapped in scent, curried, marinated, and conserved. Here we're all in the broth together, buyers and sellers, sauté-ed in spice and oil. We're peppers strung on a single cord. I know everyone; everyone knows me.

A young man reaches down from his perch atop green beans: "Mama! My bean. Very pretty. Fresh. How many you want?"

He touches my shoulder, but someone else—an older man, wizened face, half his teeth—grins and grabs my elbow: "No, Mama. Mine! How many?" They laugh; I laugh. I'm bowed to, shoved, gently pulled and tugged through the fruit.

"How many? Very cheap!"

I reach for a cucumber, a pineapple, a bunch of bananas; whatever I reach for, "No, no—not that one, Mama. This one, Mama. Better. Fresher!" and the perfect specimen is pulled from the bottom of a pile, from behind a display.

"How much?" I ask.

"Two thousand five hundred T-shillings." I hand over three thousand and the girl scrambles to make change.

"No, keep it," I say. I've just paid $2.50 for six tomatoes, two potatoes, a cucumber, and a bag of fresh peas.

"Bless you, Mama!" I move on.

Already I've gotten to know my favorite vendors here by name— Tomato Mama, Baba Cucumber (he'll throw in a green pepper if I buy more than one cuke), and Avocado Lady (hugely pregnant, and I wonder each visit if she'll still be here). Most speak as little English as I speak Swahili (almost none), but I point and hold up fingers. When I show them a handful of money, they take what they need. Food is so cheap that even if they gouge this *mzungu* twice over, it's a bargain. I know they need the money.

The main structure here dates from colonial days under Germany. It's a football field in size with about a hundred different cooperative stalls, each little stand loaded with produce in five- and six-foot piles. Avocado Lady sits on her towering green pyramid. A kanga covers her girth, but beneath it, I can see her knees spread wide, and her expanding bulk hangs between them. I think of how tired she must be in these late stages, swollen and probably bone-sore. She's not that young, and I wonder how many children she's already birthed. A young boy hovers nearby to run her errands. If I ask for tomatoes and she doesn't have any, or if I need change, he'll fetch them from another vendor. Will the boy take over her job altogether? That baby must be coming any moment.

"Mama Mzungu! Jambo!" She grins and leans down to greet me. I rush over; if she loses her balance, we'll have an actual cabbage patch kid. I hold up four fingers, and she searches through her pile for the best specimens. When I hand over twice the T-shillings, she gestures to the boy, but I shake my head.

"No, you keep it." I smile. She smiles. I've just purchased the biggest, tastiest avocados in the world for less than a quarter apiece. She's just earned herself enough money to feed her whole family today.

In the Central Market, I feel like I'm in the real Africa. Africa, Africa, Africa...there's more than one. This one is noisy, thronging, and entrepreneurial. It's black and white splashed with pure color, no nuanced shades of mauve here, no grays or taupe.

It doesn't take long before my basket is full. I've added avocados, peppers, carrots, onion, pineapple, a small melon, a bit of rice, and a bag of fresh cashews. My attention switches to the surrounding *dukas*, tiny little open-front shops, each specializing in its own wares. There's one for stationary, one for kitchen utensils, etc. Mixed in are *dukas* for cell phones, cameras, and electronics. This is the African answer to the American mall, but with an amalgam of time periods. Take away the cell phone booths, and you'd swear you were standing in the middle of a prior century.

A dressmaker's *duka* has the blue print fabric I want for making sofa pillows. I buy enough so I'll have leftovers for a wall hanging. I choose a stack of Iringa baskets from another. Two hand-carved giraffes and an elephant find their way into my bag too. Earlier in the week, I'd informed Russ that our house needed decorating. He'd rolled his eyes, "Oh, Mama...," but then he'd good-naturedly helped me drag the heavy furniture around where I directed it. I'd also brought in some house plants.

That occasioned some grumbles from Cosmos, "Why Mama want plants in the house?" but he'd helped me get them potted.

I'm approached by a young man selling maps. He's an independent dealer with a curious mix of goods: maps under one arm, decorator pillows and mirrors under the other. A burlap bundle tied on his back bulges with more treasure; I see cutlery handles poking out. Behind him is a small child he's obviously using as pack animal. I said independent, but I'll later learn there's really no such thing; these young hawkers work both for and against *dukas* and cooperatives in symbiotic eco-political relationships inscrutable to the *mzungu*. This one speaks vendor English. "Mzungu! Mama, you buy? You need? See, big of Tanzania!" he says as he unfurls a three-foot wall map of his country. I need. All our walls are white and bare. This will be mounted over our dining table.

"How much?"

"Thirty thousand T-shillings."

"Too much."

"What you give me, Mama?"

"Hmmm." I take the map and pretend to examine it for authenticity. My sense of direction is so poor that if on this map north were down and south were up, I wouldn't know the difference, but he doesn't know that. Or maybe he does and he's just playing a game. "Twelve thousand T-shillings?"

"Twelve thousand? NO!" He pretends outrage, and I begin to walk away.

"Okay, okay, Twelve thousand. You tough, Mama!" We both have what we wanted.

Russ shakes his head at me. "Mama D! Indeed, you tough!"

On this particular shopping day, if I could have projected myself into the future, I would have seen my map seller and me becoming unlikely friends. He'd find me any time I ventured downtown. The second or third time we met, I asked his name. "My name is Mbatta," he offered with a formal bow. But then, "You remember easy because it sounds like 'Mgotcha'!" delivered with raucous laughter at his own joke. Russ would tell you that, indeed, he got me every time!

Over the months, I bought his original wooden carvings (not very skilled) and learned that he kept Dickens's *Great Expectations* by his mattress for night reading. His goal was to one day become a medical doctor, but first he had to finish secondary school and get to college. I bought aprons and placemats, hand-sewn by his wife Beatrice (also not very skilled), and learned they were raising four children, two of their own plus two nephews orphaned by AIDS. The day he told me, "Please, Madam. My family has no food," I bought a dozen batik pictures.

I hadn't divulged where I lived, but he knew. I was hiking up the hill after a market trip, my arms loaded with a full basket of produce, and he popped up from behind the giant boulder at the last bend. "Ah, Mama, you have bought much *chakula* today." He mimed putting something into mouth as he reached to carry the basket. "*Nyanya, tango, ndisi, pilipili...*" [tomato, cucumber, banana, pepper]; he listed what he could see. Besides being my personal vendor, Mbata had taken it upon himself to teach me Swahili.

We reached my gate. I called for Cosmos to open and let us in, but when he saw who was with me, he balked.

"Mama, this is not proper. He should not come inside."

"Cosmos, it's okay. He's my friend."

"This kind is not to be trusted, Mama. I am here to keep you safe." Cosmos had definite ideas about what was "proper" and not "proper." We'd had disagreements. It wasn't proper for a woman to leave Wilolesi unaccompanied. It wasn't proper for a woman to drive a car. It wasn't proper to visit the Hillside alone or let the neighbor's children beyond our gate or feed the stray cat. I took Mbata's arm and directed him past Cosmos, through the backyard, and into the house.

We stood in the kitchen, and Mbata looked around. I put my groceries away while he ogled. This was something amazing. To begin with, the kitchen was inside, unlike typical Tanzanian cooking areas. It had an electric refrigerator, electric burners, and a sink with a cold water tap. Incredible. Marvelous. Such luxury. "Mama, you are blessed!"

For just a moment, I'll project myself into the future even further. Three years have passed, and I've returned to Iringa with a group of friends. Mbata still recognizes me. But our relationship has taken a different turn. After the first effusive shouts and hugs, each of our meetings feels a bit desperate. There are no more conversations about what he dreamed for his future or what he hoped for his family. There are no language lessons. The humor is gone, and I notice that he looks older and a little gaunt, as if he's been ill. He hounds me, sometimes even lingering outside our motel, waiting for me to emerge. "You have friends, Mama. You make them buy from me."

The last time I saw him was the day before I left Iringa. Our group was boarding a bus for one last excursion when I felt someone grab my arm from behind.

"Mama, there is not much time. Today I have pictures. Very good quality." He untied a bundle wrapped in old newspapers. Inside were the ubiquitous batiks of "typical" African life, designed for tourists looking for the exotic: elephants, zebras, kanga-clad women with baskets on their heads, Maasai warriors, and baobab trees. I reached out to finger one; they were greasy, still full of wax, sticky with dust and newsprint. I couldn't help but think they looked as shopworn as Mbata. "How many you take?"

My protestations were ignored. "No, Mama. There is no more time. I will leave these with you, and you will decide how much." He rolled the whole thing up and shoved it into my arms, then turned and was gone.

I felt weighed down and by much more than those fifty or so greasy batiks. They were my responsibility, but so was Mbata. Physically he'd disappeared from my life—I never saw him again—but his heavy sadness penetrated my being.

Before I left Iringa I gave money to our innkeeper with directions that it was for Mbata. Whether or not he got it, I'll never know. The batiks went back to New Hampshire with me where they were sold in a church auction, the money earned to benefit our congregation in Isimani.

One of the batiks hangs near my desk. It shows four stylized African warriors dancing around a fire, wild hair lit by flames. I like to think those warriors, replete with the satisfaction of a successful kill, share the essence of the smart, optimistic, quixotic Mbata who stood in my kitchen one day saying, "Mama, you are blessed!"

But it's not yet the future. For another few weeks, Mbata will be known only as Dot's Map Man. Tonight we'll dine at the BKB apartment on more of Grace's spaghetti and tomato sauce, and Russ will regale the Fultzes and the Langnesses with stories about our day. We'll describe scenes and share anecdotes, and we'll talk about our favorite market people. As the night wears on, eventually the talk will turn back on ourselves, our weaknesses and vulnerabilities as we attempt to fit ourselves into Iringan culture.

Because the day was spent mostly at the market, talk will focus on the local economy. We American Lutherans aren't the only foreigners here. Over the last decade, Iringa has become quite international. Being at the convergence of two major highways makes it a stop-off for southern travelers on the way to the capitol, Dodoma. Its proximity to safari parks makes it a point of departure; its historical significance makes it a destination in its own right. Several universities bring international scholarship, and businesses from India, the Mideast, and China proliferate. Our conversation on this night will expand to encompass globalization. It'll wax and grow into considerations of international fiscal equity and supportive governmental policies. We'll touch on education and medicine and electronic communication and business infrastructures. As we help ourselves to third and fourth glasses of wine, the talk will finally ebb back into the space where it began: our specific place in the Iringan universe. We'll wonder at our small responsibility here. We'll look over the items we bought at the market and wonder who took advantage of whom as we haggled over those meager purchase prices. Disparities between the American and Tanzanian economies make our pittance seem their fortune. We can easily afford to take a gouging…but only after allowing them the dignity—and amusement—of the fight.

In the end, as we bid each other good night, we'll acknowledge what we knew all along, that they know us a lot better than we know them.

7

Church

Warning: The following paragraphs may not be suitable for all readers in that they include mature language.

Ash Wednesday, Russ and I drive down the hill to attend the evening service at Iringa's Lutheran Cathedral. On this holy night, we know it will be filled to capacity, that Bishop Mdegela in all his regalia will preside, and that multiple choirs will provide musical jubilation. We arrive half an hour before the service. Already the sanctuary is crowded. Squeezing into a pew halfway toward the back, we find ourselves squashed up against a group of women and young girls. A pretty diaper-clad baby is perched on the knee next to mine. My grandmother eyes identify it as not yet a year old, probably about nine months. I whisper, *"Zuri sana!"* to the woman holding it, and the baby reaches out to touch my strange white skin and hair.

Directly in front of us is a row of teenage girls, chattering and giggling like teenage girls, passing notes back and forth and examining the contents of each other's purses, like teenage girls. The one seated directly in front of me wears a hot-pink T-shirt that reads "Gilmington MN" across the back. That's not unusual; American cast-offs are seen here all over.

I expected choirs and jubilation, dancing, drumming, maybe tambourines and other percussion instruments. What I didn't expect is electronic cacophony, instruments and accompaniment piped through music systems that put our puny little New Hampshire church system to shame. The front chancel and choir areas are filled to capacity with pastors, evangelists, and various personages of importance, leaving little room for musicians, so as the hour for service nears, singing groups seated throughout the sanctuary rise in place to perform—and I do mean *perform*. The sound is deafening: throbbing through the bones 'til feet just gotta dance. Choreographed routines get the congregation moving, and soon, even this timid American Lutheran is clapping and swaying. The sanctuary is rockin',' and the actual service hasn't yet begun.

The girls in front of us rise to perform. They bump and grind, a little J-Lo, a little Beyonce, all energetic arm pumps and bootie. They whirl to face us. I can now read the front of hot-pink-Gilmington's shirt: "If you want to celebrate whorehouse days, you have to have a few pricks." I glance at Russ to see if he's reading what I'm reading. He is. The look of surprise on his face matches mine. We've seen secondhand T-shirts imprinted with American sports teams and company logos around Iringa, and they always give us a jolt, but this one is an out-and-out shocker! We Americans have the audacity to think that our garbage is always a useful and welcome contribution to African society. I'm guilty. I drive up to that big yellow depository bin behind the gas station, open my trunk, and heave plastic bags stuffed with unwanted clothing—last season's styles, outgrown, the wrong color choice or just plain superfluous—and I think I'm being altruistic. Tanzanians call these items "dead *mzungu* clothes." Why else would someone throw them away?

Whatever song was being sung, whatever the lyrics, I was no longer hearing. I was lost in reflection, trying to envision how this young girl came to be advertising that message. First I imagined myself watching the girl at home, envisioning the moment when she grabbed that silly hot pink shirt from the closet to wear to Ash Wednesday service. She'd probably pulled that shirt out of a bundle of used clothing thrown from the back of a lorry downtown. Perhaps school had just let out for the day, and she and her girlfriends were ready to let off steam. They detoured through the marketplace on their way home. The two young men unloading the lorry had called out to them, baiting them, gibing and swiveling their hips.

70

"Hey baby! Pretty ladies! Come have a look!" They giggled, and the girls began pawing through the pile. The hot pink color caught her eye first, and she hugged the shirt to her chest as she ran off with her friends, laughing and breathless from exertion and exhilaration. They ran down four streets, across the park, through the traffic circle, dodging a motorbus and collapsing on the steps under the clock tower where they sat to compare their loot. Together they read the message, giggling and pooling their skills at American argot until they caught its meaning. When she went home, she hid the shirt and thought about it.

It's hard to be a girl in Iringa, especially if you're poor, and doubly if you have aspirations. A girl doesn't have the same advantages as boys. Unless your family has money, your future isn't expansive. Education is valued, but your brothers' schooling takes precedence. If your family can't afford your tuition, you're sent out to find work. Entry-level, low-paying positions—bargirl, house girl, construction crew attendant, etc.—usually come with "fringe benefits." In addition, the surrounding poverty, together with the convergence of two major highways, makes Iringa a ferment of prostitution. Of course, Iringa isn't the only place where this happens; it's global. But here, where the HIV/AIDS infection rate among adults has soared to an astounding 16 percent, it's devastating.

The Tanzanian Lutheran church has taken on HIV/AIDS education and relief as a main cause. Many praise songs include verses about healthy living and practicing safe sex. It's quite probable that the girls singing in front of us on this holy night are singing the lessons of abstinence, but I don't hear the words. I'm focused on why the girl chose to wear her shirt tonight. Is it as a joke? Is it for shock value? Teens around the world appreciate shock value. I choose, however, to believe that her implications might be deeper. My experience so far in getting to know teenage girls attending Tumaini is that underneath the silliness, the madness inherent in adolescence, is a mature and unvarnished purposefulness toward life. She knows all the above. Perhaps in wearing the shirt, this young woman is turning her body into a social statement.

I choose to applaud this brave young woman. And the Lutheran Church in Iringa. When the song finishes, I stand with the rest of the congregation, applauding and cheering. If I knew how to ululate, I would.

My mind is spinning. It's no longer in this worship space but rather back home in America delivering university lectures on the struggles of residual colonial society. I'm interrupted when I hear my name announced from the front. My bombastic reverie must wait. "xxxxxxxxxxxxx—Dr. Dot Kasik—xxxxxxxxxxxx." One of the pastors is looking at me, beckoning. The bishop, standing beside him, acknowledges me and gestures that I should stand. I stand. Applause. I wave my thanks and bend to sit. The pastor walks toward me, madly gesturing now. I am to come forward. Obediently I walk toward him, and he mouths to me in English, "Introduce yourself. Say a few words." And so I face the congregation, tell them my name and explain why I'm in Iringa. I look to the pastor and he motions that I should say more. I give the congregation greetings from my home church in America and glance at the pastor. *More motioning.* So I launch into a full description of my first Tanzanian trip three years ago and how it changed my life—*more motioning*—tell something about where I teach in America, how it relates to what I'm doing at Tumaini, how the Internet makes for global educational connections no matter where we are—*more*—a listing of the members of my family back home, how much I miss them, which of them are coming to visit and who have already been here—*still more...* Everything is translated into Swahili by the pastor. Finally he turns to shake my hand, holding onto me while he speaks to his congregation, no doubt explaining to them the reasons for whatever *faux pas* I've been perpetrating while standing up here.

I go back to my seat.

The baby now decides to crawl into my lap. She's wet; baby pee seeps into my skirt. I feel a sticky thigh. Ugh. She scuttles across onto Russ's lap. He unwittingly cups her bottom with his hand; a look of surprise appears on his face. Gently but firmly, he hands her back to my lap and surreptitiously fishes the antiseptic bottle from his pocket.

Something that I love about Christianity in Tanzania: no boundaries, no separations between everyday life and the worship service. Everyday life gets dragged into the service, played out in front of the congregation. Sure, the children are dressed in their best (usually their one and only dress for little girls, the only white shirt and miniature tie for little boys, passed down from brother to brother or sister to sister), and they're certainly on their best behavior, but there's a transparency and physicality on display that doesn't happen in the States—breastfeeding while singing in the woman's choir; chickens and farming products brought and presented during offering. Tanzanian life being played out physically, realistically throughout the service. Christianity is life: we should take that message back home to our fellow New Hampshire Lutherans. Christianity is life. And to these folks, the church service itself is life.

Iringa is a population of the churched and the mosque-d. Whether Muslim or Christian, Tanzanians are serious about faith. Many of our students are very open about their religious life and affiliation. Tumaini being a Lutheran university, most profess Christianity; still, it is not unusual to see women's headscarves among the group, and on Fridays, the Muslim men come to class wearing their white robes, ready to attend worship. In New England, where I live most of the time, thinking about religion and living one's faith requires effort; we're the most unchurched region of America. By contrast, in Tanzania, church is the fabric of life. Life weaves itself through religious expression. You can be Christian or Muslim or a tribalist—or a combination—but in Iringa, unless you're a foreigner, you both profess and practice *something*.

In Wilolesi, I wake to the *meuzzin's adhaan*, the mysterious Islamic call to prayer, from the neighborhood mosque, and I mark the end of my day with his final appeal. Sundays open with the cacophony of church bells. Christian structures abound, from the traditional cathedrals of the liturgical to auditorium-sized megachurches to nondenominational storefronts. Mosques appear every ten miles, some ancient—like the clock tower marking the middle of town—but others newly planted. The majority of social services—schools, orphanages, craft centers, medical facilities, and a host of

NGOs—are sponsored by religious organizations. Here in Iringa, I'm afforded respectability by my association with Lutheranism. It's a marked difference from at home in New Hampshire where personal faith is often greeted with more tolerance than enthusiasm, or at my university where belief in a being higher than science can be down-right suspect.

After our cathedral experience, our friend Hellen from Tumaini's administrative offices invites us to attend Sunday services at her Pentecostal church.

"Please, please, please, please, please *come*!" Hellen does every-thing in a high mode of excitement and with *style*. Our first day on campus, after the ridiculous faculty meeting where we'd just been given teaching assignments, Happiness had been sent to show us to our new office in the legal corridor. She handed us a set of keys and wordlessly disappeared. While we stood fiddling with the lock, we were interrupted by a tinkly, high-pitched "Hello-o-o-o-o!" from across the hall.

It wasn't what we expected. This particular hello was suggestive, sensual, spicy—certainly *not* collegiate. It was, in fact, out-and-out sexy. A lissome young woman leaned from the doorway opposite. She stretched one arm up along the doorframe, reaching out toward us with the other, waggling her figures. "I'm Hellen!" she warbled. "I'm here if you have any questions. Any questions at all. I'll probably know the answers!" Her tiny dress and dangerously high stiletto heels complemented the voice.

Hellen, it turned out, is a bit of a chameleon. The next time we saw her, she was wearing a business suit and solid shoes. Another day, a curly red wig complemented a flowing skirt. Her wardrobe—and shoe collection—is as varied as it is endless. We wondered at the size of her closet. Russ and I soon took to daily speculations about which Hellen we'd be seeing.

Not to worry. Hellen *told* us who she was: "I am the person who will help you the most." And she did. In our first confusing weeks at Tumaini, it was Hellen who showed us around and answered our questions. In her dual capacity as accountant to the dean and graduate student, she understood more about Tumaini's inner workings than most folks. If we had an administrative question, Hellen answered it. If we needed supplies, Hellen knew where to get them. She took us to the faculty lunchroom, told us which food to order, and showed us how to pay the bill. Hellen knew everyone. She introduced us to useful people on campus, the "chalk lady" who handed out teaching materials, the IT person who handled computer complaints, and the cleaning ladies. When I complained that my students hadn't read their assignments because they couldn't access certain texts, she showed me how to put books on reserve at the campus library. The first day I received notice that a particular student was removed from my roster because of unpaid fees, she introduced me to the college bursar and the registrar.

All this was done with unrelenting good cheer, and everything was punctuated with "the-name-of-Jesus-Christ-my-Savior." Hellen is unmarried, in her early twenties, and lives with her seamstress mother (hence the huge wardrobe) and two unmarried sisters. An older brother teaches in Iringa secondary school. Hellen's father is dead, but he left his family with a house in town. Owning a home decisively categorizes them as middle class, but that classification never guarantees enough to cover extras, let alone practicalities like utilities and school tuitions. Sometimes even food is scarce. The family operates on faith. Every morning before Hellen leaves to catch the *daladala* for Tumaini, Mama makes her kneel to receive her blessing.

She's been asking us to come to her church and meet her family for several weeks. We want to, but most Sundays we're expected to accompany the BKB team to services at one or another St. Paul partner congregation. A free Sunday has finally arrived.

We follow Hellen's directions and find ourselves in the parking lot of what we previously thought was an industrial warehouse. Corrugated metal marks the outside walls, but once we're inside, we see the space has been transformed. The walls are decorated with fabric hangings and Christian banners: GO PREACH CHRIST and HOLY SPIRIT POWER and BE RECONCILE. Potted plants and flowers line a dais where card tables and lopsided lecterns hold Bibles and microphones. Electrical wires string from the ceiling. Almost all remaining floor space is covered with metal folding chairs and moveable pews.

We swarm in along with hundreds, perhaps a thousand, fellow worshippers. A glance around us reveals that we're the only white people here. People press from all sides. We're surrounded by black, engulfed really, despite of our whiteness or because of it or maybe both. Ushers take our arms and guide us to front rows. Hellen brings her family to be introduced, her mother—who'll spend the next three hours on the dais—two sisters, the brother, various cousins, uncles, and "aunties." Hellen's immediate boss from Tumaini, Professor Seth, comes to greet us. I am surprised to see him here. I'd taken him for Lutheran, not only because he heads a department at the school but because I knew he'd spent a year as visiting professor at a Lutheran college in the States. Hellen and her family and Seth greet us in English, but it's the last we'll hear all morning. We'll be immersed in Swahili, but it won't keep us from being thoroughly and religiously entertained.

The service begins. Professor Seth seats himself among a half-dozen clerical-clad men on the dais. Without liturgy, without a Lutheran format, it might be hard to follow, but as the service progresses, I get caught up. Everything is done at high decibel. Preaching is shouted. Scripture is shouted. Prayers are shouted. I determine each by delivery: Preaching is eyeball to eyeball, accompanied with sweeping arm movements, jabbing the message home. Readers hold open Bibles, stabbing and punching the Word. Prayers shout aloft, stretching arms to the ceiling. Ecstatic calls come from leaders and congregation alike. A spontaneous dance breaks out, and I'm pulled to my feet. We snake through the aisles and gyrate before the altar table. Tongues break out, wild speaking, wild screaming, and crying. Women ululate.

The lead pastor comes down from the dais into his audience and touches a devotee on the forehead. She keels over, slain in the Spirit. Down goes another, and another. Ushers position themselves throughout the auditorium to deal with the passion, ministering to the affected as necessary. Frenzy ebbs and flows in waves.

But no one can sustain such energy for long. A calm descends, and someone delivers a sermon. A collection plate is passed. Another person in clerical robe speaks, and this time it sounds like a scolding.

Again, the collection plate is passed. Another sermon—another collection—I lose count.

At the end of three hours, we're tired. When Hellen invites us to come to her house for a meal, we decline as politely as possible, assuring her we have far too much course preparation that must be completed this very afternoon. We go back to Wilolesi and collapse.

As already alluded to, the usual Sunday experience was to tag along with the BKB folks to one of the seventy-three St. Paul Synod-Iringa Synod paired congregations in rural Iringa District. None of the back roads we traveled ever made directional sense to me. Don or Gary would be at the wheel of the Land Rover with Pastor Msigwa from the diocese riding shotgun, and we'd race over dirt tracks through bridgeless wadis, snake through nameless villages, sometimes picking up passengers along the way, and arrive where we were expected, exactly on time, which is to say, any time before noon. The morning service won't begin until we arrive. The scenery always left me breathless. We might be in deep wooded valleys, on a heart-stopping precipice, or wandering through desert, sometimes all on the same trip, and always with the Udzungwas towering in the distance.

I've never been car sick, so I don't know the misery. But folks not used to riding in a vehicle often have trouble. One morning a pick-up passenger lost her breakfast. She was covert about it, vomiting repeatedly into her voluminous *kanga*, each time folding to hide the mess. She was so quiet we'd never have known but for the smell. When we arrived at our destination, the car was spotless—nothing on upholstery or carpet. We left the windows open.

When we arrive at the village, it's always Palm Sunday. A throng meets us as we turn down the road toward the church. The women dance; the men wave branches or pieces of colorful fabric. Children jump around with glee and abandon as we're paraded into the churchyard. The wild welcome song, *"Karibu! Karibu!"* rings with gusto. As we park and embark, it's into waiting hands grabbing from all directions.

We're escorted to the parsonage for more songs, formal prayers, and breakfast served by the pastor's wife and her women friends.

Breakfast is *mendazi* (fried donuts), *chapati* (flat bread), boiled eggs, tea, and Coca-Cola. Without fail.

And then it's time to worship. We're led to the sanctuary with more singing and dancing, and we're seated near the altar as guests of honor. Either Don or Gary will preach; within a few weeks' time, I know each of their sermons well. They speak in English while Msigwa translates.

Pastor Msigwa represents the Tanzanian face of Bega Kwa Bega. He's funny and caring, passionate about what he does, and dramatic. When Msigwa translates, the congregation gets a theatrical review of scripture. Zaccheaus, for instance, climbs the nearest altar rail tree to get a better look at Jesus. Abraham takes his imaginary staff in hand and wipes his brow, arduously making his way across the sanctuary desert. A wedding guest at Cana twirls in ecstasy as he tastes the wine, and the woman at the well balances a tipsy water bucket on her head. Msigwa plays all the parts. I've seen Gary laugh so hard at Msigwa's antics that he has a tough time finishing his message.

The first Sunday that Russ and I drive out alone to worship at Isimani Lutheran, we don't realize all we're getting ourselves into. The morning begins as we'd come to expect, complete with Palm Sunday welcome and parade. Pastor Chaula is expecting us. He ushers us into the parsonage where we find the entire church council waiting for prayers and breakfast. I'm well into my second *mendazi* when Russ asks Chaula, "Pastor, what are you preaching on this morning?"

"Oh, well…" Chaula says slowly. He wipes his hands and motions for the women to bring more tea. He coughs. There are another several moments of silence. Then, in a tone one would use on a small child, he explains, "You see…it's something like this. The guest is always invited to preach. You will be able to do that, no? Which one of you will preach?"

Russ blanches. Obviously, as the male, he's the one expected to volunteer. I gulp and say, "We'll do it together."

Three minutes panic, three minutes' preparation, and we're ready to go, taking our lead from our mornings with Msigwa. The Gospel for the day is the story of Jesus forgiving and redeeming the woman about to be stoned for prostitution. First Russ plays the part of a Pharisee, waving his whip around and fomenting the crowd. I play the crowd, obediently fomented. I switch into the role of the woman, sobbing and cowering. Russ morphs into Jesus, offering his hand and sending me off in peace. All of this takes up considerable time because everything has to be explained and translated as we go. Chaula does the translation. The congregation snickers and pokes each other in the sides; they high-five and jump up and down. I hope the laughter is *with* us rather than *at* us. After we finish our dramatization, each of us "preaches" for about five minutes, explaining what we've personally learned from the day's Gospel and how it might affect our behavior or increase our faith. Then I sing a song and we're done. Baptism by fire; now we know we can preach.

On a regular Sunday, when we're not in Isimani and not expected to sermonize, we still have to introduce ourselves and bring greetings from the States. And then we're given gifts—clothing, jewelry, a bag of eggs or peanuts, a jar of honey, dried corn and beans, the occasional chicken or goat.

My first gifting of a chicken pleasantly surprised me. I like chickens. I tucked the bundle under my arm like a kid with a teddy bear. It squawked loudly and began to fight. For safety, all but the neck and head were secured in a plastic shopping bag, then wrapped in a *kanga*, so the fight was loud but ineffective. I clucked back at it and scratched its neck. It calmed immediately. "Chicken whisperer!" someone murmured. Maybe. Instinct bubbles from some deep memory; I'd picked eggs from the time I was four.

The presentation of the goat presented more difficulty. That too came during a Sunday morning service. The goat was used to being around people, and he just wouldn't stay put, making his way from person to person, shoving his nose into places better left unexplored. I had him by the rope around his neck, but I wasn't strong enough to curtail his activity. Finally one thoughtful congregant came to my rescue and took him outside for the remainder of the service.

Gifts must be accepted with appropriate thanksgiving and grace. Refusing a gift, even a rather difficult corporeal one, would be an affront. Clothing and jewelry are joyfully accepted and worn, food stuff easily used. Live chickens are regifted in Iringa to native

Tanzanians who have no compunction against turning them into their next meal. As I mentioned, the goat presented more difficulty. Even a squawking chicken can be endured inside the vehicle; not so a goat. My goat was trussed and tied and fastened to the Land Rover's roof for the drive back to Iringa. It didn't easily comply. The entire two-hour drive was accompanied by piteous bleating. The poor beast was understandably terrified, and apparently when goats are terrified, they defecate. Every jolt from the road brought a fresh shower of goat turds past the windows. By the time we reached Iringa the vehicle was plastered.

Tanzanian church services easily stretch to three hours. Each of several choirs needs to sing. Then there are often several sermons and lengthy readings, prolonged processions, and remarks by visitors. Various offerings are taken, money or whatever else people have to give. Over the weeks, we saw baptisms, confirmations, and services of reconciliation. At one service, five people spontaneously came forward for baptism—two Muslims and three Maasai. If it's a Eucharistic Sunday, communing takes an additional hour.

In the States, once the blessing is given, everyone is ready to go home. Not so here. First, there's more singing and dancing in the churchyard. Sometimes there are dramatic displays, fire dances, for instance, or Maasai jumping contests. Then everyone gathers for the weekly auction. Remember the offerings? Items are held up one by one, and bidding ensues. Eggs, baskets, honey, fabrics, and creatures find appropriate owners; the money they bring in is added to the locked offering box. (At one church, a man turns to me to explain the auction: "This is the American part!" But nothing about it registered as American to me.)

After the service, we return to the pastor's home for lunch. The women have butchered and prepared a chicken—*kuku*—along with rice, beans, mustard greens, spaghetti and tomato sauce, and white bread (because this meal is too formal for *chapati*). Sometimes there's goat meat too and *always* Coca-Cola. Finally, we meet with special committees to discuss well digging, corn donation, school operations, or other projects shared among the BKB partnerships.

By the time we make the bumpy ride home, it's dark.

On Sunday mornings, I experienced much that was holy and much that was wholly inexplicable. I know of no other way to describe it but as an expression of the ineffable. That God deigns to share His holiness with us is privilege beyond understanding. It's manifested in so many ways, mostly rooted in the people themselves: A crowded congregation parts like the Red Sea as a dozen Maasai warriors, brand-new converts to Christianity, choose to come to the communion rail for the first time. A rural sanctuary fills to the point that people have to stand outside at the windows to listen. A young mother openly nurses her infant while singing in the choir. An elderly man's face glows with holy joy as he plays his treasured plastic recorder, dangerously off-key.

Nothing could have been more holy than the first evening I spent at Matebete. When a government holiday closed the university, Russ and I had a few days off to travel. We asked the Fultzes and Langnesses to recommend a place to visit, and in a chorus, they said, "Matebete." The Lutheran Diocese and BKB routinely hire Maasai warriors as guards and drivers. Already we'd gotten to know Matebete's Papili, the guard at the Lutheran Center, who especially loved watching ESPN soccer with Russ in the Center lounge. We knew Kulwa, one of the Diocese's drivers. Anna, Eliada, and Tulizo, my students at the university, were Maasai from Matebete as well. Russ and I were eager to visit the place we'd heard so much about.

Our good friend Peter, the same Peter who'd been our savior that first night in Dar es Salaam, would now drive us to the village and serve as translator. Early on Friday morning, he drove the now familiar van through our Wilolesi gate to pick us up for the four-hour drive. Cosmos glowered. We'd been lectured at relentlessly over two days after telling him where we were going. "Professor Russ, the Maasai are not good. They cannot be trusted." When he saw Russ wasn't changing his mind, he turned the appeal toward me. "They all have many wives, you know, but a man there doesn't even live with his wives. Mama, the men will bother you." In the end, when he saw how determined we were, he told us he'd be praying for us, beat his hand against his heart, and begged us to be careful. As Peter drove us through the gate, he stood blocking it, making one last appeal. And then finally, backing down in complete frustration, shaking his head and murmuring, "Jesus Christ in my heart, Jesus Christ in my heart," he let us pass.

Hours later, we veered off the main road and stopped at the edge of a heavily wooded area where two tall Maasai men emerged from behind trees and boarded the van. From this point on, there would be no discernable roads, only trees and the thick, undisturbed underbrush of the compound where a *mzungu* would immediately be lost. From here on, we would be in Elia's and Nateo's hands.

Matebete is a government-sanctioned reservation where the Maasai have freedom to live out their traditional culture. The community lives off the land, raising goats and cattle and sleeping in cattle-dung *bomas* built by the women. They practice strict time-honored separations of sexual roles, living and eating with their age groups rather than as family units. Today the children wear uniforms to attend the government schools built onsite to educate the children. Today the district representative elected from the village dresses in Western clothes to go to work. But at the end of the day, everyone changes back into traditional clothing, men in *shukas* and women in blue or purple *kangas*, both in extravagantly beaded silver jewelry. They live mostly without electricity or running water.

While they may be resolutely traditional, custom doesn't prevent them from being enthusiastically entrepreneurial as well. In a small clearing in Matebete's center, surrounded by acacia and evergreens, they've built an adobe guesthouse to accommodate a dozen "tourists." It's furnished with bunk beds and mosquito nets. Across the yard, a second adobe building bears a hand-lettered placard reading "Matebete Café." The café features a nonworking Coca-Cola machine, two tables without chairs, no kitchen, and no food. Behind the complex is a state-of-the-art outhouse with two separate compartments and shower facilities (buckets with hoses).

Perhaps at another time, in another chapter in another book, I shall write about all that happened over the next extraordinary forty-eight hours. I'll talk about being shown the government well dug for the Maasai cattle and describe how Elia lifted me to stand atop a boulder when Peter translated to him that my father had been a dairyman. I'll describe the haunting, guttural droning beneath the men's songs and the high, nasal answering chorus from the women as they danced beside a bonfire at night. I'll talk about how Nateo jumped higher than anyone else in the jumping contest and how everyone cheered and laughed when Russ finally agreed to join in. I'll tell about thousands of silver disks and how they glinted like sunlight on ocean water as the women danced, about the women's purple dresses flashing in the moonlight, about the flirting and sensuality displayed in the dance. Finally, I'll tell about sitting under the stars around the bonfire for evening conversation, about the way the men marveled over Russ having a mobile phone that could produce the Internet, and about their eagerness to understand our lives in America. I'll close my paragraphs with Peter's translation of Elia's final question to us: "How does it happen that in a country with such a history as America [slavery], a black man with a Kenyan father is elected the forty-fourth president?" But for right now, I'll skip over how amazing it felt to be chatting under the stars with two dozen Maasai warriors in a secluded compound deep in the heart of Tanzania, because what I need to describe is something even bigger. I need to tell about my moment of theophany, God breaking through and revealing the Infinite.

My childhood was spent mostly on farms, which means I've seen a hatchet hit the chopping block as a chicken struggles against the hand holding it down. I've seen the blood spurt as head separates. More than once, from behind a shed, I've listened as gunshot ended a life, then watched as the carcass was hoisted up, slit, drained, and carved into steaks. On each occasion, I felt the strange mix of horror and fascination at brutal spectacle.

And so when Elia, as head *moran* of the community, directed us to the place where we would witness the killing of the goat in preparation for our feast, I steeled myself against revulsion. There was none.

The goat was a *sacrifice*. I watched, and I was overcome. Surely what I was seeing must have happened in the Old Testament temple. Here Elia was the priest, the forest floor itself the altar. Before the act of killing, Elia ran his hands comfortingly all along the goat's back, feeling its life, calming it, assuring it of its importance and value. He said what sounded like a blessing—it probably was—before he slipped a noose around its neck, threw the rope over a thick branch of a sturdy tree, and pulled. Nateo and two other men joined him on the rope. Within seconds, the goat hung limp, the life quietly gone.

The goat was laid on the grass. Then Elia took his knife and deftly, smoothly, with one long stroke, slit the skin from chin to chest, belly to testicles. Gently, he laid it back, slipping the blade between skin and muscle, folding it into a smooth white leather blanket along each side. There was no blood yet, and the underbelly was completely bare. Then after arranging neck skin into a pocket, he slit the carotid just enough for the blood to pool. Laying his knife aside, he scooped a handful of hot red sentient blood and drank.

Russ and I watched wordlessly. I glanced his way once to gauge his reaction, but I couldn't read him. He was in his own world. Elia, still kneeling, turned and offered for Russ and me to drink. Russ declined. I declined. I wondered even in that moment: was I giving up something precious? Cheating myself? One by one, the others in the crowd, thirty or so men, both young and old, came forward, knelt, and drank. My world rocked. Time disappeared. Place disappeared. There I stood in a wilderness in Africa, watching an unbroken chain of holy tradition, the drinking of animal blood as the fulfillment of holy command, understanding no more and no less than millions over millennia engaged in this one singular awful and beautiful sanctified act.

I have since that moment never gone to the communion table without seeing a Maasai man kneeling to drink the blood.

Three years earlier than my Matebete stay, I had learned that at Isimani Lutheran, where a large number of Maasai had become members, the *morans*—though officially they'd professed Christ and joined the congregation—refused to attend worship or take communion. They sent their women instead. All that changed the first time that the American partner congregation from somewhere called New Hampshire came to visit. All Isimani had heard we were coming, even those who never set foot in the church building. On the Sunday of our actual visit, as the worship service progressed to the Eucharistic moment, a dozen Maasai warriors in full native attire, machetes at their sides and staves in hand, appeared at the rear door. Silently, as if on command, the ocean of people parted to make an aisle. It was the biblical story, except that these peoples had no pharaoh's army in visible pursuit. The Maasai walked single file down the center, straight to Pastor Linn—the American pastor—to receive the bread and to drink the blood of Christ.

Holy moments are unexpected. They sneak in. It's impossible to prepare. We're never ready. Theophanies will forever be mysteries, things that we know to be true but are unable to either fathom or explain.

Mostly they happen in the humblest of circumstances.

8

· ◆ ◆ ◆ ◆ ◆ ·

Layers

Halfway through the semester, there was the moment I looked in the mirror, and my whiteness surprised me. It was late afternoon, the end of a long teaching day, after more than a few long periods of gazing out over a sea of chocolate and coffee, of kicking back in the lunchroom with chestnut, of chatting across the administration counter with ebony, and crowding in at a library reading table elbow-to-elbow with sable. And now I'd come home to change my clothes and freshen up before meeting folks for supper. I grabbed my toothbrush and bottled water, went to the sink to spit, looked up, and saw a ghost—chalky skin, white hair, pale eyes.

The African sun had deepened my complexion several shades, but I was still a pasty-faced Norwegian. I think because these folks had accepted me, offering their friendship, poking good-hearted fun at my frequent cultural *faux pas*, I had begun to believe—sometimes—that I was one of them. But I wasn't.

There had been an illustrative moment earlier in the day, and now that I turned it over in my mind, it bothered me. We were sitting in the faculty dining room, my friend Hellen and I, and across the table were professors Michael, Seth, and Falres. Falres was explaining the faculty trip he was planning; Seth recounted a personal tale from last year's trip; and Michael spoke excitedly about going along this year. They looked at me. "You'll come too, won't you?" I asked what sorts of accommodations were being arranged and how much it would cost, and the entire table broke into Swahili, obviously checking with each other about what to tell the *mzungu* and effectively cutting me out of the conversation. Seth made some sort of joke; they laughed. Michael looked at me, grinned and nodded, and returned to the insider conversation. I could have ignored it all, but Hellen put her hand on my arm in what felt like a compassionate gesture. It was disorienting. In the middle of inclusion was also exclusion.

To live in Africa as a Westerner is to live within layers of acceptance and behind gates of separation.

On a daily basis, I felt both intellectually and educationally confounded in a dichotomy of concurrence and alienation in the classroom, but there was even more in my personal life. Western rules of social correctness or good manners sometimes failed me. I often felt I'd fallen down Alice's proverbial rabbit hole, where displacement from the usual was disorienting. Where was I? Who was I becoming?

Holed up in my bedroom at night, I'd try to puzzle things out in my journal while listening to the night sounds. I heard hooting from a sad and confused owl in the backyard, the questioning wind, and the mournful baying of the neighborhood dogs. Maybe I was anthropomorphizing, endowing all sounds with my own befuddlement and loneliness. Night sounds tend toward the mournful. In those moments, my mind would often settle on visions of the Maasai camping in Uhuru Park, the ones who probably slept under the stars and who weren't readily accepted in Iringa's polite society. I heard the night guard just outside my window, shuffling around to get comfortable in the chair he'd dragged up onto the front porch, expectorating, bunched up in his old ragged jacket, sniffling against the nighttime cold. I felt safe behind my wall. And I felt alone.

The journal was a farewell gift from friends before I left the States. Its first few pages were covered with handwritten messages. "Safe travels!" "Stay safe and healthy." "Enjoy the adventure and return speedily to your friends." One stood out from the rest: "Be your Viking self, explore." It was signed by my Scandinavian friend Margareta. I thought about the Vikings in my distant past, convinced that they had a lot in common with the Maasai.

Curled under my mosquito netting with a tiny booklight, pen in hand, I was determined to scribble my way toward sense. I could go on for pages, sometimes hours, lost in time as I probed, sifting through the day, holding new experiences up against former attitudes and opinions. The new didn't always fit with the old. Things didn't always match up. Old layers were being scraped away and new layers applied.

On this one night, my musings are interrupted with sounds coming from the lot next door. There's a house under construction there, and I've been tracing its progress. I know the workers leave midafternoon, so sounds this late at night are worrisome. I'm hearing metallic scraping, then there's a bang like a metal pail being thrown. Someone is definitely on the lot, someone who doesn't belong there. Whoever it is obviously isn't concerned about discovery because they're making too much noise. I'm not frightened, just very curious. I turn off the lamp, get out of bed, and creep to the window.

Wilolesi is pitch-black at night. There are no streetlights. It's early enough so that the sky is still clear and a little moonlight seeps through. By midnight, rainclouds will obscure everything, but now I make out outlines and shapes—our wall, a couple of trees, and the new tile roof next door. Our night guard is investigating too. I watch him creep along the wall up the slope of our yard to the point where he can just barely see over. I see him holding something in his outstretched arm—a gun? I wasn't aware he was armed!—and then a flash of light. He's "armed" with a flashlight.

The faint beam traces a path over the stones, into the still-empty windows of construction, and over the rooftop where it catches the outlines of two big old male baboons. A third animal pops up from below onto the wall at the guard's head. Instinctively, he reaches out and whacks the creature with his flashlight. The baboon screeches. The beam catches teeth bared in an unholy grin, and guard and baboon each fly back to their respective sides. Our guard creeps back to his shack. The marauders aren't deterred in the least, and the banging and clanging continue. I think they're playing catch with something metal. I creep back to bed.

I've been watching the building of this house with interest. As it emerges, it's teaching me to understand more about our own house. When completed, it'll overtake ours in size considerably although ours is large by Iringa standards. We have three bedrooms and two baths, an indoor kitchen with electric appliances, a large dining room, and a sunken living area with fireplace and powder room to the side. A *mzungu* from America might think she's living somewhere in the States until she notices that the kitchen stove is an electric two-burner atop a table; that there's no oven and that the refrigerator dates from 1950; and that taps throughout dispense only cold water. Nevertheless, so long as she's safely ensconced within these walls, there are times she can almost forget that she's living in the third world. Then just as she's surprised by the whiteness of her face in the mirror, the subtle African architectural differences bring her up short, reminding her gently but consistently that things are unfamiliar. Are the differences important? Can they teach her something? Do they really matter?

Twice the size of ours, the house next door is huge. I've watch it grow day by day. The first time I saw it, workmen were laying concrete blocks, placing them directly on the ground without the area being leveled beforehand. I can surmise our house was built the same way. Our lot slopes toward the street, so the room farthest from the road, the kitchen, is highest in elevation. Next in order comes the dining room, one step down. Closest to the street is our sunken living room, the sinking of which has little to do with elegance but everything to do with the ground beneath being lower. And so I navigate a stylish four steps down to sit in front of the fireplace. From the midlevel of the house, I step up to the hallway, up again to my bedroom, and down two for the bath. Russ steps up one to his chambers, up again to the bath. Were a third person living with us, the route to get settled for the night would be up-one, up-another, down-one, up-one, down-one, and up-one. I review my own route in my mind before each midnight bathroom run.

How different this is from residential construction in America, which usually begins with some pretty serious excavation. My husband and I have added onto our old New Englander several times, and each project began with digging a really large hole. The hole took a long time, having to be carefully squared and leveled with accommodations made for plumbing and sewage before the concrete subflooring was poured. A lot happened beneath ground level and behind the surfaces, and when the main floors and walls appeared, all that early stuff was hidden away. Conversely, there's little hidden beneath the surface in a Tanzanian house.

"I'm living closer to the earth here!" I wrote one night. "From room to room, my feet follow the natural lay of the land." Literally, the terrain was hard to ignore. I began to think about how *grounding* this was. I'd not experienced this much grounding since running barefoot as a child. It felt good. It felt...authentic. "Everyone lives closer to the land here," I wrote, "because you're always interacting with it: dirt floors, dirt roads, dirt walkways..."

"Back home in the States," I continued, "I pack on layers of insulation to separate and protect myself from authentic terrain. Whether my 'terrain' here is physical or philosophical or even spiritual, Africa is teaching me to give more attention to what grounds me."

The next day in the Tumaini Library, I searched out Paul Tillich, the German philosopher. I remembered spending a semester as an undergrad with his philosophy and finding new spiritual awareness for myself through his theory of God as the "ground of being." I found him in the religion section. My fingers brushed across titles: *The Protestant Era*, *The Shaking of the Foundations*, *Dynamics of Faith*, but those weren't what I was looking for. I wanted the work my professor had said was Tillich's introduction of theology to a general readership. I searched, to the end of the shelf, down a level, then up. And suddenly there it was: pay dirt! *The Courage to Be*. I took my prize to a quiet corner and began to read.

"...It is the expression of the experience of being over against non-being," he wrote. "Therefore, it can be described as the power of being which resists non-being." Huh. You'd think that if an eighteen-year-old read those words, she might have been led to lead her whole life more thoughtfully grounded rather than having to learn the lesson slightly past middle age.

I'm back to watching construction. Over the course of the weeks, walls have materialized. The main building is taking shape, two stories, multileveled, and expansive. It's going to be fine looking. One day I see a man drilling straight through the wall near ground level, once, twice. Next I see the point of a drill emerging from behind the walls up on the second story, once, twice. I'm intrigued and decide to investigate. When the work crew clears out midafternoon, I venture over. The property is left unguarded, so I wander at will. I walk in through what I surmise will be the back door and find I'm in the kitchen. I know because a kitchen sink, drain, and piping are laid out on the floor, and just above them is the first hole. The holes are for pipes! Laying concrete flooring directly on ground leaves no space beneath for water or sewage. So I learn that plumbing is ignored until concrete walls are erected and fixtures are located. Then holes are cut through as necessary to accommodate them. In our house, pipes carry toilet waste to an outdoor cistern, but sink water simply drains back through the wall to a pail outside where it's collected and carried to the garden. Electricity is handled the same way: cut a hole for the wire, string the wire through house where it's needed, then box the wires out of sight. Like building to hug the terrain, the method for connecting utilities is simple, straightforward, and perfectly adequate.

Straightforwardly constructed as needed, with nothing extra. What if I tried constructing my life that way, meeting my needs as they arise instead of worrying and overplanning for eventualities which may or may not materialize? I realize I spend a lot of time fretting about the future. Again, in my journal…

"The lack of foundation means no basement storage space," I reflect. "Come to think of it, no attic storage either." For the average person here, personal property is so limited that storage is unnecessary. I note how I came here with what I considered the bare minimum, and to date, I haven't needed or missed anything. I have so many possessions in America. Material possessions, but nonmaterial as well: too many hobbies, too many grudges, too many opposing ideas, too many unhealthy habits. Suddenly I find that having less in the way of the material frees my mind to also let go of the mental.

Here in this house, there aren't even closets. When I need to store something, I use a basket or a box. Oh, that my entire life were that easy to organize!

I learn a third concept: dump the unnecessary. Live simply.

Okay…so these three concepts—being more grounded here (closer to God, more conscious of God) and living more faithfully (less fretting about the future) and simplification (fewer possessions): now, how do those realizations help with the uncomfortable feeling of separation, the tension between belonging and exclusion. Am I talking about layers or about walls?

Certainly, at the very least, they're examples of things that confuse and confound me. And teach me…when I take the time and make the effort to parse them.

So I take my ground of being and my living in faith and attempt to apply them to other questions. My white skin in the mirror was just the reminder that I am and always will be different, that there will be separation. Separation isn't bad. I need to learn to accept it and negotiate the space between.

The laughter from fellow professors in the lunchroom came because my first question, my first impulse was to be concerned with the costs, accommodations, and transportation for an educational safari. Exhibiting those worries showed my layers of cultural extras: the trappings of worldliness and the cover-ups such trappings elicit in a foreign culture. The particulars were obscuring what was important. And that's always the Westerner's first response: worry about the particulars.

From my bedroom, I have a good view of my front yard, the driveway, the wraparound porch, and the guard house. That's because there are two banks of windows here at the corner of the house. Each of the panes of glass in these six windows is a different size. The frayed curtains hanging from rods above each window are each their own length, some shorter than the window frames, some longer. The rods themselves are hung at individual heights with a collection of brackets and bent nails.

My bed is positioned beneath one bank of windows. The mattress is the usual size, that is to say, the usual Tanzanian size. Mattress sizes here are standardized, either single or double. Whichever, they're rolled and strapped to the back of bicycles to be transported home after purchase. Bedframes are calibrated by a different yardstick altogether. Mine, for instance, is a double, but it measures six inches longer than the mattress. The linens provided by Tumaini include two flat sheets (six inches shorter than the mattress, a full foot shorter than the bed) and two blankets (even shorter). To keep the mattress in place, I use the empty space at the end of the frame to store my backpack, a book bag, and a laundry bag. Handy.

If bed frames and mattresses don't match, neither do many other groupings. Windows are almost always installed in threes, but each of the three is a different height. Curtains packaged as sets are assorted lengths.

I notice more discrepancies. In a single staircase, each riser is unique in elevation. Doors and doorframes within the same house, within the same room, vary in dimension. Our six wooden dining chairs are six distinct heights, and the slats in their backs vary in width. On our sofa, each of the three cushions is a different length and bulk from the other two.

But while individual items are rarely of standardized *sizing*, almost everything available for sale in the marketplace is standardized in *design*. Chairs, for instance, can be counted on to be constructed of wood, stained a medium oak brown, with five upright slats across the backrest, the backrest itself at an angle to discourage relaxation. Sofas are built with wooden frames in a style Americans used to call "colonial" in the '60s. This doesn't vary. In fact, in all of Iringa, in all of the homes, government offices, or motel lobbies I ever visit, I only ever see a single model of chair and one version of sofa. And the cushions never fit.

Inconsistencies in measurements and order are everywhere. Sometimes they're glaringly obvious; other times they're subtle, just the sort of differences that trip up an unsuspecting Westerner who anticipates consistency. I fell one night on the concrete steps leading down from the BKB apartment, scraping up a wrist and bruising a leg, because my foot had expected evenly calibrated risers.

A friend hired a local electrician to install sconces as reading lights in her bedroom, one on either side of the bed; one turned out three inches higher than the other. I look around my bedroom and see the same effect with light switches, outlet plates, even the faucets above my sink, the cold an inch higher than the hot.

Thinking about the neighboring construction, I notice that history counts. To understand these homes, I need to take in their construction history, what natural forces and circumstances shape their manufacture. I surmise it's the same with culture, and so I begin to review what I know of Tanzanian history.

In a sense, Tanzania is everyone's homeland, as evidence of the earliest hominids are found here, the footprints of whom were uncovered by Mary Leaky in 1978. Europeans from several nations trekked through during the nineteenth century, notably Henry Morton Stanley and David Livingstone. Tanzania's southern mountain range bears Livingstone's name, as do a dozen of my students. He is revered here. His body lies in London's Westminster Abbey, but his heart, removed by his native attendants, is buried at the roots of a tree in Zambia. A moving memorial in Zanzibar honors his fight against the slave trade.

After Livingstone's death, in the last decades of the century, Germany systematically took control and colonized both Zanzibar and the area known as Tanganyika. Specifically, Iringa was established as a military base, which both you (the reader) and my students know because of Mkwawa's legacy. All those Germans needed places to live, so Gangilonga and Wilolesi, the hillside areas flanking the town, became white neighborhoods. The real Iringa was nestled between—*crushed* between—and dominated over by the German government and business buildings that distinguish Iringatown even today.

Then the World War hit. Germany suffered defeat, and the colonizing of Tanganyika was handed over to Great Britain. That's the way things stood until Tanzania—Tanganyika plus Zanzibar—gained independence in 1964.

Independence changed everything. President Julius Nyerere, the George Washington of Tanzania who hangs on every classroom wall, declared several things: that there would be the brotherhood of Tanzania instead of tribal living, that Swahili would be the national language, that English would be the language of education, and that education would be free and public through elementary school.

"Africa is still such a dichotomy, so much a struggle between worlds," I scribbled one night. "Everything 'modern' is right in front of us. And yet. Lush soil with up-to-date agricultural techniques, but women still working in the fields, digging with their hands. Big rigs and road equipment, but women with 100-pound loads on their heads and babies on their backs. Computers and cell phones, but it's impossible to mail a letter."

More questions, and these of the practical variety that hit me every day: Why is every shower curtain hung on wires instead of poles? Why is the wire crooked? Why are no two walls straight? Why are all walls in the new construction next door plastered over to cover the supposedly ugly brick, but nowhere is the plaster smooth and even? You'd think with all the practice that Africans would be the finest finishers in the world, but they're not. It's a bit like Cosmos putting all the work and energy into our gardens. New beds, prolific feeding and watering…and in a few months, we leave and it'll all go to seed yet again or dry up from lack of rain. Why not garden instead with dry spells in mind?

Once on an earlier visit to this country, I'd voiced my frustration with these sorts of contradictions to an elderly pastor friend, and he'd said, "So why do you feel as if you have to understand Tanzania? Just let it wash over you." I tried to recall his words of wisdom now, but I was finding it was easier to let things wash over me when I wasn't living in the midst of them. If you're going to live here as an American, I was learning, some things have to be let go: matching stair risers, tidy paint jobs, smooth roads, finished buildings, coordinating window curtains, and blankets that fit the bed.

Could there be something deep within the African mind that refuses to comply with the expectations of the West? Are their "inconsistencies" a way—albeit unconscious—to rebel at the hundreds of years of having foreign systems imposed upon them, of having their tribal life destroyed? What if outsiders stopped interfering, stopped giving so much advice, and let them work out their own systems... and maybe that's precisely what Africans are doing.

I began developing a theory. "I'm speculating about the results of all that colonialization," I mused. "Its remnants are everywhere. Its effects permeate all Tanzanian experience from furniture design to German buildings in Iringatown to the structures of government. English trumps Swahili, and British legal and monetary systems dictate. Tanzanians struggle to be their own proud people." European and American cultural systems are adapted, bent, interpreted and reinterpreted. "Can it be," I wondered, "a sort of underground rebellion? Were—are—the inconsistencies a method of conforming by nonconforming?" The irregularities don't bother the Tanzanians, but they drive us Westerners mad. They trip us up and cause us to make our own adaptations. I remembered Elaine, the former Wilolesi tenant, showing me the nail holes from where she tied a string across the bathroom door to remind herself in those midnight trips to pee that she had to step down; the string was stretched at face level to hit her nose a millisecond before her foot forgot to plan for the descent.

Are the contradictions mere superficiality or something deeper entirely?

I had no one with whom to voice my theory. How does one frame a question about subversion without risking offense? On what level would the question be interpreted, and—even more complex— on what level would the answer come?

Finally I took the chance and broached the subject with my friend Tuti, manager of the Iringa Lutheran Centre guesthouse and a good friend and resource to BKB. I asked whether or not my theory had any validity, and she said, "Yes." There was a definite line of subversive thinking that she felt could absolutely be traced back to the time of colonialism, but that now it was so ingrained, so endemic as to be subconscious. It was "just the African way." Tanzanians are actually surprised when the inconsistencies are pointed out. They're so ingrained that they're invisible. It's unfortunate, she said, because what began as a subversive tactic has now turned against them. Whereas it used to be to trouble the waters, to punish, to confuse, to addle, or to make awkwardness for the colonizers, it now thwarts

African efforts. "Westerners see these things," she said, "and think we're stupid or, at best, careless."

On the contrary, in their own society, they're more sophisticated than the foreigner. They may well align themselves more closely with the natural world, but that's hardly a lack of technological acuity. I have only to think about cell phones to know this. Tanzania developed a mobile phone culture long before we did, and that's because they were smart enough to skip over some of the developmental hoops we went through in the States. In Tanzania, a reliable connecting telephone service never existed—the infrastructure simply wasn't here—so the entire nation connected itself with mobility. Mobile phones hang from every neck. You can buy a chip or a card in even the remotest of villages. When the Maasai slaughter a goat, the leather provides two sheaths, one to hold a machete and one to hold a cell phone. No one in Tanzania today is deciding whether or not to give up a landline because there never was one.

Mobile phones aside, sometimes it's as if they live mostly on the edge of modern amenity, looking in with enough clarity to see things as they might want them to be, but still not having the technological infrastructure to access them, and occasionally even when the technological structures are there, social ethos gets in the way. I suggested to Lotte Chuma at Tumaini one day that the college should purchase a couple of push mowers so that the groundskeeper women wouldn't have to cut the grass with machetes. With a look that implied that I had two heads, Lotte's response was, "But then these women wouldn't have jobs."

I think Tanzanians are inventing themselves. It's not my job to decide who they should be. In truth, it's not my job to even understand them. If I deign to know how best they should operate, what Western habits they should adopt, what amenities they need to procure to be like us, that would represent colonial thinking at its worst.

So long as I live here, every time I look at myself in the mirror, my face will always be the same, that of the *mzungu*, the different one, the foreigner. That fact may indeed present some uncomfortable contradictions between me and them, but it's okay. I can acknowledge that our individual interpretations of life, how we approach problems, and how we respond to exigency come from places deeply cultural and deeply historical, and neither is good nor bad. Just different. I am who I am; they are who they are. We can laugh at each other and at ourselves. Even in their laughter, my experience is that they're always, always, *always* kind. To wit, Hellen's gentle hand on my arm is true compassion, both acknowledgment and assurance in the face of difference.

When you deal with dual cultures, you might try to play a matching game; but it's a trick. There are no exact matches. I can imagine that Tanzanians who visit America are no less confused by our culture.

I open my journal. "Be your Viking self; explore." Okay, Margareta. Agreed. I will.

9

✦ ✦ ✦ ✦ ✦

Invitation

Friday afternoon, Russ and I are getting ready to abandon the Guest Professor Office when we hear Falres's "Hellow, hellow!" For me it's been a trying classroom day at the end of a trying week; Falres's appearance is welcome.

We love and admire this man. Always cheerful and encouraging, the sort of person hopeful in the face of hopelessness, he makes things happen simply by positivism. Falres always has a new idea. Today's idea: inviting two American professors to join his faculty tour.

He stands in the doorway, composed in his normal—formal— stance. "It will be the second of its kind for Tumaini."

For a split second, I relive my discomfort in the lunch conversation a day ago. I wonder if his invitation is an attempt to make up for whatever those three men were talking about, why they were laughing at me.

"My intention is that it will be a time of cultural erudition for our professors," Falres continues. "It will also bring our faculty together in social ways that have not yet been explored. Success will lead to a desire to repeat it every year. You will be part of creating a new tradition. What a wonderful opportunity it will be for us to have American professors along."

We peel the bags off our shoulders, throw them back on the desks, and invite him in. It sounds intriguing.

"There will be forty-four of us," he says, and he interrupts himself to shake hands, first Russ's, then mine, holding my arm and locking eyes as he resumes. "Students, faculty, and administration. Five days. Through the Southern Highlands of Tanzania, all the way to Lake Nyasa, which is, of course, as you know, called Lake Nyasa by Tanzanians but Lake Malawi from the other side."

Falres always manages to sound professorial, delivering the archetypal lecture. He drops my arm and stands erect in the center of the office. By contrast, Russ has taken a chair, leaning back a bit; I perch myself on top of my desk, resting my feet on the seat of my chair. When it occurs to me that my stance might appear disrespectful, I stand and clasp my hands in front of me.

"This sounds quite wonderful," I venture. "How will we get there? Do we need to arrange transportation—purchasing tickets, for instance. And what about hotel reservations?"

"And how much will it cost?" Russ gets right to the point.

"I will answer those questions in a few moments." Obviously, we've interrupted. Falres has readied a presentation for us, and he's going to deliver it, regardless of our poor manners. We listen.

"I will begin by telling you that my ancestors were from the Kinga tribe, and I was raised in the Kinga tradition. Thanks to the first president of this country, Julius Kambarage Nyerere, we are all the Brotherhood of Tanzania rather than individual tribes, but we can still talk about and find value in our histories. I have therefore designed the itinerary for this tour to introduce you to something of Kinga culture, both past and present." Falres continues his spiel, but I'm finding it difficult to concentrate. My mind wanders to the towering pile of work on my desk. I had saved a lot up for this five-day semester break. "I have a lot of work…" I begin, but he holds up a palm. I'm silenced.

"I have arranged that we will tour two medical facilities," he continues, "one very modern and one a traditional birthing hospital. I will introduce you to a traditional mountain home. We will enjoy presentations by cultural experts on dance, film, and music. You will see firsthand how our young people are being trained to deliver messages of healthy living. Historical sites will be included."

I have several hundred student papers waiting to be read and graded. I have lessons to prepare, reports to edit, and grades to file. I have a midsemester exam to be written. Now Falres suggests I ignore it all and travel. How African, I think. In America I'd spend all five days shoulder to the wheel, nose to the grindstone.

Russ speaks, "I'll have to think about this. My wife Jo arrives in a couple of weeks, and I want to be able to take some time to spend with her. I have a lot of work to complete…"

I agree. "I was counting on our break time to catch up…"

Falres is not deterred. "There's always time for work. This is the time for cultural travel." He has a point there. "We may even venture into Malawi itself, at least just across its border. I am sure you would like to report to friends and family back in America that you have been to that country as well."

"But what about the cost?" Russ tries again. "We aren't all made of money, you know." My own bank account is dwindling. I begin adding the costs in my head: five days of transportation, five days of meals, four nights of lodging, a few entry fees along the way.

"There will be opportunities for you to shop as well!" Falres nods toward me. "Local artisans are in abundance, for example. Lake Nyasa is famous for its pottery." He waits a moment to let it all soak in.

"Now to answer your specific questions." He relaxes his stance and smiles. "The university is providing vans and drivers for our excursion with no additional cost to you. Overnight lodging will be in Lutheran Centers, and meals will be prearranged. There is no additional cost for presentations. I will be your tour guide. Having said all that, it may be a bit expensive. I realize you might be on a budget, but I think you will find it well worth the investment. Yes, certainly you will."

"And the exact cost?" Russ asks.

"75,000 T-shillings."

A five-day excursion through the Southern Highlands, the Livingstone Mountains, and Lake Nyasa for 75,000 Tanzanian shillings. In US currency, that's approximately $55.

We're in.

10

✦ ✦ ✦ ✦ ✦ ✦

Falres and the Faculty Tour

In the end, fourteen of us set out on Thursday morning. Our grouping was brilliant, and whether or not it was ultimately engineered by Falres, we couldn't have been more wisely chosen. We were a wild mix of teachers, students, and employees—American, European, and Tanzanian. From the professorial community, the group included Michael from Tourism; Jan from Anthropology; Falres and Sally's husband Paul from Theology; and Russ and me from Law. There was a professional photographer—we'd all be starring in promotional films for the university—and a couple of administrative assistants. We were each about to be plunged into serious research. Whatever we saw or heard would be thoroughly examined, interrogated, unpacked, scrutinized, cogitated over, and evaluated. Anyone—me—who might have thought she was on vacation was mistaken.

As we packed ourselves into the two Land Rovers, Falres directed even our seating arrangements. "Dot, you will sit in the second seat in the center, next to Karen from Minnesota, behind Sally, also, as you know, from Minnesota. Gloria will sit on your right. You can talk about what you see, and Gloria can answer your questions."

"Yes, I am Gloria." She was gorgeous. A star Tumaini third-year tourism major, she would soon prove herself both patient and brilliant.

Our friend Dani was at the wheel. Falres had suggested rather strongly that Russ should find a seat in the other vehicle.

And so we were off. Leaving Iringa, we headed south and west, from the top of the Southern Highlands over into the heart of Mbeya, into Falres's Kinga territory.

The aim was to be introduced to Kinga culture, therefore, to an earlier and more rural Tanzania than we'd experienced in Iringa. Falres's educational philosophy found expression in the similarities and differences among traditional Tanzanian religion, secular tribal culture, and modern Tanzania, particularly academic Lutheran Tanzania. Our five-day expedition would meet those goals. He promised we'd be introduced to both people of power (political and religious figures) and "real" people (commoners); we'd enjoy special presentations, visit historic buildings and shrines, see contrasting medical facilities, enjoy the Livingstone Mountain scenery in its various forms both by car and on foot, and finally end with two luxurious days at Metema Beach. Whew. Pretty ambitious.

The Southern Highlands of Tanzania are dominated by what most Iringans call the Livingstone Mountains but officially renamed the great Kipengere Range, according to modern maps. This is the eastern escarpment of the great East African Rift. From Mbeya the range stretches south to Lake Nyasa, where lake country people call them the Kinga Mountains, perhaps the most fitting of all, since tribal Kinga have made their home here for a very long time. The Kinga are traditionally agriculturists—bananas, bamboo, wheat, potatoes.

The terrain here is dramatic and erratic. Each mile is a new experience. One moment we were negotiating a steep grade with hairpin turns, the next a plunge into narrow abyss. Along the roadsides, heavy vegetation hid homes and smaller settlements from view, but we knew they were there because the roads were crowded with foot traffic. In some places, the hills were rocky; in others, deeply forested. And then in an instant, the scenery would open up on a great steep swath of green. It might be bamboo covered, or it might be golden wheat. Some glittered in sunshine; some were shrouded in mist. On every surface, people lived and farmed the way they had for years, for eons and eternities. It was beautiful contour farming, the kind I thought we'd invented in America's Midwest. Graceful, curving rows of vegetation hugged spectacular vertical tracts. We saw no heavy machinery, no tractors, no plows, no bulldozers. Everything was done by human hands wielding hoes. The workforce climbed effortlessly up and down slopes like Sherpas without snow.

The driving was wild and dangerous. Roads were in extreme disrepair. A pothole could be as large as a VW, and there might not be a way around it. Occasionally, we'd meet a logging truck or a lorry that took up most of the road, and we'd edge to the side and wait. When we came up behind one, we held our collective breath. The loads looked precarious. Logs were held on with delicate chains that seemed more like necklaces than restraints. One broken link and a single log would easily crush an SUV packed with academics.

We'd drive an hour or two, and then we'd stop. Our days were punctuated. Midmorning might find us at a cultural center presentation. Lunchtime we'd be entertained by musicians or dancers or regional commissioners. Midafternoon would find us trekking along into a valley to view a cave or a lake or a statue. Suppertime would find us yawning through a political speech, our stomachs growling, supper itself postponed till a later hour.

But then evening would fall, and there would be respite. I never stopped being amazed that in the midst of all the wilderness and activity, at the end of the day, a Lutheran Center would appear, usually the hospice for a secondary school. It would have real bedrooms, mattresses with clean linens, flush toilets (enclosed but open to the stars), running water for showers (albeit cold), and a buffet supper. European Lutherans had been busy establishing churches, schools, and hospitals throughout Mbeya since the midnineteenth century.

Late in the afternoon of our first day, we pulled over to a small adobe house nestled in at the base of a mountain. "You will now meet my old professor," Falres told us. "I will go first. Then if he's able to see us, I will call you. He is old and frail. Please greet him with respect." Which meant each of us would murmur "Shikamoo, Babu"—which translates something like "Respect to you, Grandfather"—and bow our heads a little as we were introduced. Crammed into our seats since lunchtime, we stumbled gratefully out to complain about sore muscles, compare notes about the day, and await our summons.

Already today we'd been through Ifunda, Mafinga, Ihefwe, Mbalamasiwa, Idofi, and Makambako. From there we drove to Kimani and Chimala. Their names were like music, and indeed, we heard music everywhere we went. Singing hosts had served breakfast, simple bread and tea at a Lutheran Center. Lunch had included a musical presentation from SUMASESU (Support Makete Self Support), an NGO established to facilitate sustainable development. It had been an elaborate affair in a traditional dugout, six steps into the ground, under a grass roof. Our presentation featured teenage dancers in elaborately feathered costumes. There was live drumming to a thunderous electronic sound system, wild gyrations, and acrobatics. A film and lecture about SUMASESU's work followed, punctuated with more dancing.

The day so far had been a multilevel onslaught. I had given up trying to take notes after the first two lectures, promising myself I'd look up SAMASESU on the Internet later. The musical cacophony had spent my emotions. I was physically spent as well; it's surprising how tiring it is to be immobilized. Now, released from our vehicles, we scattered while we waited. Russ took off on a short run. Paul and Sally spread their maps out on the ground to trace our route. Michael sacked out in the grass, fedora pulled over his face. Gloria, Karen, and I kneaded each other's backs.

It was a full hour before Falres brought the professor out with his wife. The old teacher wore the traditional *kofia* on his head; he was stooped but spritely. A tiny wizened woman, head wrapped in the same fabric as her *kanga*, clung to his arm. Both were balanced on canes. As directed, one by one, we offered obeisance and trundled inside, the taller members of the group ducking heads at the doorway.

The house was the usual two rooms, one larger, one smaller. Outside stood a storage shed and the privy. Standing now in the main room, I looked around and decided that for this old, venerated couple, it was appropriate. I saw no evidence of electricity or running water; no appliance, no sound systems. Cooking would have been accomplished outside on kerosene. I imagined their lives, appointed and decorated with people rather than things; it was sufficient.

Shoved up against the rear wall was the ubiquitous plaid-upholstered divan, with wood frame and embroidered doilies. Two chairs flanked it. The professor, his wife, and any guest who might come to visit (a former student, maybe) would sit side-by-side staring out the front door at the mountains, sharing the same perspective. A low table stood within easy reach, a humongous Holy Bible resting on its end. I imagined food lovingly prepared to share. On the wall above the divan hung a faded Obama poster boasting "From Kegelo to USA President." In a front corner stood the remains of a Christmas tree. A Christmas tree. It had been pine, perhaps a decade earlier. Silver tinsel still dangled from a couple of its bare branches. It bespoke memories of pleasantness. I could imagine that not too many years ago, they'd held a festive celebration, with a guest list of family and former students. The food would have been special—*kuku* and *ugali*, tomato sauce and beans, *chapatti* and *mendazi* and fresh fruit. To drink, there would be local beer, strong coffee, and chai. The talk that evening was loud. Someone brought a drum or perhaps a recorder; several had shakers. One of the younger boys had ankle bells, and all the youth broke into joyful, frenetic dancing while the old men clapped and the old women ululated. After a time, the old Bible was opened to Luke 2, and the Christmas narrative was read for the children.

I could imagine all this because all the talk was in the local dialect, musical and faintly hypnotic. I stood leaning up against the wall and let my tired, overtaxed mind wander. My thoughts drifted around Falres Ilomo and the paths he must have taken to get to now: ordained Lutheran minister, respected theology professor at Tumaini, author, international scholar. Thinking about everything he's accomplished makes me wonder what I've done with my own life. He's not a physically large man, barely taller than I am and slight of build. His face is pleasant but plain. The carseat-creased purple suit he had on today was the only thing I'd ever seen him wear, always with dress shirt and tie, and always with stylish, pointy-toed dress shoes, spit-shined to a mirror, and worn even for hiking. Still, there's something about him that commands respect. I studied him. Whatever he was saying must have hit a nerve; the old teacher reached out to stroke his cheek. Falres covered the teacher's hand with his own. I liked their private moment.

"And we will now go on to our next activity, climbing the mountain just there." He pointed left, slipping back into being tour guide. "It is a slight ascent. When we're halfway up, we will stop and observe an interesting monument. Those who wish to keep on going will continue over the ridge where the climb is more difficult. Others may decide to go back down the way we came." We were herded outside and onto a mountain path leading into deep woods.

I remember nothing much about the hike up and nothing at all about the supposed monument, only that we were in a heavily forested area where the line of sight was limited. The view ahead was rocks and trees; the view behind was rocks and trees. It was not unlike mountain hikes back in New Hampshire.

At the monument, Karen and I decided to attempt the trek down without the others. "Yes, it will be easy," Falres assured. "Just retrace your steps."

At first we were moderately confident of our path, but then after the first hundred steps or so, rocks, we'd memorized as distinctive on the way up began to look surprisingly consistent on the way down. We'd come to a fork in the road—and there were many, none of which we'd seen on the way up—and had to decide which to take. Nothing looked familiar. Quietly we talked about how far we may have strayed from our original route. A sliver of fear made me breathe a bit slower, but we kept going. Sometimes the path was so rough that we literally jumped from one rock to the next. We optimistically told ourselves and each other that so long as we were consistently descending, we couldn't be far off the path. The deep woods made it impossible to see beyond a few feet in front of us.

And suddenly we weren't alone. There was a man running along beside us, crashing through the undergrowth, diving between trees. We'd barely had time for his presence to register before he'd jumped out onto our trail and planted himself in front of us. He looked savage, dressed in pants tied with string, a torn shirt and old plastic flip-flops. Bloodshot eyes oozed with pus, and unctuous black frizz snaked to his shoulders. Without warning, his eyes locked on mine, and he leaned in so close I could smell him, acrid, pungent, fetid. As he reached toward me, I drew back in a mix of fear and revulsion. He laughed and shook his head. "*Hapana, hapana!*" No, no, he wasn't threatening me, only gesturing with black boney fingers for me to follow. "*Malipo,*" he crooned cunningly as he raised an eyebrow, then turned and ran ahead. I grabbed for Karen, and we linked arms. If he attacked, he'd have to take us both.

He was mercurial. One moment he'd be galloping on ahead, the next he'd turn and beckon. Trying his hardest to get us to follow, he'd veer off onto side trails, once stopping to bow graciously with a sweeping invitation to deviate course. Jumping from rock to rock, jogging along in front of us, then hiding and jumping out from behind a tree, he was feral, frenzied, and—frankly—nuts.

"I'm pretending I don't see him," Karen said. Crazy man kept crying, "*Malipo, malipo,*" Neither of us understood the word, but his hand signals clearly begged for money.

Finally we came upon a cabin in a tiny clearing, a place we didn't remember seeing on the way up. It looked surprisingly American. A stone chimney ran up the back; neatly stacked woodpiles flanked the entrance. There were even flowers planted along a walkway. Crazy man jumped directly in front of us, excitedly inviting us to come to the yard. It couldn't have been his home; Karen and I had already determined by his looks that he lived out among the trees. We ignored his appeal, plunged ahead, and hoped he'd get the message. He was undeterred.

We veered on around the small yard and continued downward, feeling more and more confident as the descent became more pronounced. Our companion ran on ahead until we lost him from sight. And then off in the distance, we caught a glimmer of light, the sky reflected off the roof of one of the SUVs, and we laughed with relief. There was the second SUV; there was the old professor's house, the road and safety...and there were the other dozen of the group emerging from the woods a hundred yards off. We congratulated ourselves for being so clever, casually leaning against the SUV, calmly waiting for the rest to join up. Crazy man danced around us, again shouting, "*Malipo, malipo.*"

The group appeared. Crazy man made a desperate verbal attack at them. Falres turned to us. "Did you promise this man money to bring you safely down the mountain? Were you lost? Did he rescue you from danger?" Crazy, frenzied, *nuts* for sure but clever.

We were eating breakfast at Falres's mountain home the next day. I was perched on a low rock wall he'd built to surround a firepit and was sitting directly in a line of thick smoke. Falres introduced us to the two local youths he employed, and they demonstrated how to start the fire with sticks and straw. I thought of my older brother and his Boy Scout days. Smoke stung my eyes; ashes blew into my face. Coughing, struggling for breath, I pulled myself away and stood on the periphery to listen.

"The fire circle is traditional. This fire is not for cooking or for doing work. You see the low wall around it for seating, to gather the people together. At the fire circle, you bring your problems. Here is where friends meet, where the family settles disputes, and where the clan plots its future. Even more, here is where the older generation teaches the younger. This is the way the Kinga pass on their traditions."

Falres has built his vacation home in the land where he was raised, the land he still so dearly loves. It's modern, fully electric, an indoor kitchen complete with dishwasher, and indoor plumbing. Unlike his home in Iringa, this one is more overtly Western. On the one hand, it's the sort of home few of his old Kinga friends can afford, and so he's separated himself from his life here. On the other, he's built within it a sort of outdoor museum that showcases traditional values and culture. It's a reflection of his academic work, which argues for recognition, acceptance, and sometimes even inclusion of tribal belief into modern life, especially at religious points of convergence between the two. Hence, his traditional fire circle.

"Be silent. The fire will teach you. Look into the flame. Trouble is burned away. Problems become little as fire and warmth become important. What separates you from others turns out to be petty. You realize you are connected to all humanity, to all life. You are one with animals and plants. You are one with the earth, with rocks and soil and water. Time stands still and melts into eternity. You enter eternity by staring into the fire."

From the fire circle, he led us to a pair of dugouts, smallish underground rooms with entries so narrow and low they could only be attained by crawling. Carved into the mountainside, dugouts like these—one for the men and boys, one for the women and girls— would have served as winter shelters. Once safely tucked inside for the night, folks would be warmed by the bonfire built across the entrance.

Next we saw his vegetable gardens and maize field where a flock of chickens ran free. There was a pond, too, fed by a mountain spring, where several ducks were enjoying a swim while a couple of bigger fowl (turkeys?) pecked in the weeds. I loved it all. But what I loved best was Falres's goat. Ukumbusho was pure white, bred from a variety previously common in these mountains but now almost extinct. Almost everyone in Tanzania keeps goats for milking, for eating, but Ukumbusho ("a reminder" in Swahili) is a pet. She readily accepted scraps from my hand as I made her acquaintance. I ran my fingers through her long, carefully groomed hair. Such a beautiful creature. I thought how well she epitomized all of Falres's place here: something rescued and bred specifically for modern pleasure. Thus you honor and remember. Carefully perched on the mountainside, Ukumbusho and her little acre of beauty—house, fire circle, gardens, even the pond—seemed to balance on the thread of eternity.

Falres had promised us a visit to a traditional women's hospital, in fact, he said, the place where he himself was born. We would go there now. I'd already visited three medical facilities in this country on prior visits, one a modern concrete structure run by the Catholics, replete with operating theaters, long corridors, and forty-four semi-private patient rooms; and one the exact opposite with two bare concrete rooms, an empty but locked medicine cabinet, and an "ambulance," which turned out to be a bicycle with metal bed frame soldered across the rear fender.

The third, a Lutheran facility in Ilula, still under construction, had impressed me beyond words. I'd visited in 2006 with a group of Americans, and when its administrator and sole physician, Dr. Alfred, heard that three in our group had doctorate degrees, he assumed they were in medicine and had us garbed in surgical clothes for an inside tour. With pride, he showed us his operating/treatment "theater" with new (donated) equipment, featuring a Gomco sterilizer of the variety I'd used during my stint as a nurses' aid forty years earlier.

Besides the operating room, there were two ward rooms, one for women, one for men, each outfitted with a dozen single cots. Twenty-five women occupied their ward, some sharing cots, others using blankets spread on the concrete floor. Separating wards from treatment room was a tiny corridor which Dr. Alfred used as an office. A single shelf housed his library—a medical textbook and a 1972 PDR. A small table held a computer and a notebook which he opened for us, asking, "Would you care to see my surgical records?" Inside he'd carefully listed times and details of the three hundred-plus surgeries he'd performed during the year to date, a mere six months. There were routine appendectomies, heart catheterizations and valve replacements, amputations, brain surgeries, various exploratories, Caesarian sections, and more, all of which he'd performed with his single surgical nurse. We'd gasped with disbelief, and as we peppered him with questions, he smiled patiently and told us, "Whatever I am not sure about, I look up on my computer. When I have a further question, I connect with a teaching hospital in England, in Germany, in America, or in Dar es Salaam. And then I do the procedure. What choice do I have? What choice does the patient have?"

In the sunlight outside behind his facility, we found two young boys on their knees, hands deep in soapy water. They were washing condoms and rubber gloves. In this way, Dr. Alfred was saving lives.

So Ilula was on my mind as we followed Falres across an open field to the wooded area where we found the footpath to his traditional hospital. The woods were deep and dark and dank. The climb was steep but well-worn enough to be easy-going. We hiked perhaps a mile until he finally announced, "It's just a little way now, around this next corner."

Around the corner, the mountainside fell completely away. We stood on a path hugging the cliff, a single row of trees separating us from the drop. Directly ahead the track widened into a sunlit clearing tucked into the mountainside. Heavy forest umbrella-ed three-quarters of the clearing, no walls, only trees defining boundaries. Leafy branches were the ceiling. Soft earth was both bed and flooring. Two large granite boulders served as back rests for laboring women. And the sight in front of those women would be spectacular: a wide forested valley backed granite cliffs, and, off in the far distance, glimmering sunlight on water. There was a collective sigh from our whole group. If this was indeed a hospital, what patient could resist healing as she gazed at such a scene? Whatever this place was called, wherever we'd ended up, it was exquisitely private and dramatic and beautiful. More than beautiful; it was holy.

Falres smiled. "We are here."

Two small fires had been lit, one at either end. Between them stood two small, elderly Kinga women, each in traditional dress and headscarf. This was their place. They looked as if they'd grown *from* the space. Falres spoke quietly to each, touching first their heads, then their breastbones, murmuring. "Shikamoo, Mama." The women patted his cheeks, his hair, his arms. They beckoned to us. We crowded in, keeping to the edges, afraid to intrude.

What followed next was an amazing pantomime of traditional birth. Here on this ledge, in these deep woods, shielded from the curious eyes of family and public, hundreds, even thousands, of women had delivered their babies into the hands of these old midwives. Neither of them spoke English, probably not even Swahili because the next hour was rife with linguistic crosstalk and overspeak—Kinga to Swahili to English and back again, accommodating all three cultures, because birthing words—*placenta, umbilical cord,* even *labor* and *transition*—don't necessarily get included in language classes or dictionaries. Practices and customs don't translate easily either. So our questions begin to fly back and forth. Some things we hear surprise us. For instance, the liberal use of marijuana; laboring mothers in New Hampshire don't usually get marijuana to ease the pain, but they do here. Neither do our midwives get paid in corn or weed. Smoke from wood fires isn't blown into the nostrils of an infant who can't breathe. Placentas aren't buried in the ground to ensure the next healthy birth. Here on this ledge, a midwife washes her hands in aloe vera and sterilizes the mother with the same, and more aloe vera lubricates the fingers she'll push inside to check for a baby's position, change its orientation to the birth canal, or coax it along the way. When labor is difficult, an herb grown by the midwife makes the mother convulse. Another herb makes a mother who is "cowardly" [the midwives' word, not mine] vomit. Convulsions and vomiting encourage expulsion, one more drastically than the other. On the other hand, some things they explain sound or feel more familiar, like using a sterile blade to cut the umbilical cord or bathing the newborn with sterile water.

"You will see something now that few Kinga men are ever allowed to see," Falres announces. "Let us watch." He gives a signal, and now the midwives demonstrate. One lies back against her earthen pillow, spreads her legs, and tucks her skirt around in such a fashion to mimic childbirth. The second squats between her legs, pushes on her abdomen, thrusts a hand under the skirt, and pantomimes a pulling motion. They trade places and demonstrate more.

Between these two women are seventy years of practice. Each is now actively training her replacement for the community, a process that will require seven years of apprenticeship before state certification. Tanzania actually smiles on traditional birthing centers like this one. While a modern facility might be able to offer more services and more favorable outcomes, this birthing center is cheaper. The only cost to the state is a sterile razor blade for each birth. Besides the economic advantage, a traditional birthing center enjoys more respect, especially in rural areas where modern medicine is feared and women without access to a hospital end up giving birth in circumstances much worse.

Here the midwife is both feared and revered. She lives a life separated from general community affairs. If she has children of her own, they're cared for by other family members when she works. She is constantly on call. She may have a house, but she's rarely there to tend it. When she works, food is brought to her here, payment from the birth family. Once she delivers a mother, mother and baby stay in seclusion with her for two days before returning to their own homes. We watch and we listen, and we are conscious of great privilege. What we are seeing and hearing is rarely public. This place is secluded for a reason. However natural it might be, birth in traditional culture is private.

Later the same morning, Falres in the lead, we stepped single file on another narrow mountain path. Two feet wide, sometimes less, it dared my feet to find purchase. I hugged the rock, one shoulder scraping against grit, grabbing the occasional branch. Small trees grew out perpendicularly from the mountain. How does vegetation grow from pure stone? I grab repeatedly, though I know full well that a person's weight could easily uproot them. Over my exposed shoulder, the way down is easily an Empire State Building. Running along its foundation is a swift-flowing river. If I slip, I die, unless I'm lucky enough to get caught by a branch.

The path loops around and back on itself, always returning to the ledge. On the straightaways, I can see Falres still leading, bounding ahead of us like a mountain goat. He's in his element. He'd spent his Kinga childhood on these trails, and obviously, neither his feet nor his equilibrium had forgotten. In fact, all the Tanzanians are holding their own; it's I and the other Americans who are struggling. In spite of my fear, however, my Berkinstocks are performing as advertised. At one point, Russ reaches out his hand to steady me; I brush him away, more confident relying on myself. If I'm to go down, I'll go alone.

Up, up we climb; I estimate a quarter of a mile or so. Finally we round a corner and reach a level rock platform perhaps a dozen feet wide. To our backs is solid stone reaching straight up another twenty feet or so. On either side of the clearing, mostly bare trees wrestle the scree.

Still panting—more from fright than exhaustion—we gather ourselves around Falres. "And you have reached what the local people call Luganda or *Kijiua Kuweka*...the Suicide Place." No surprise there. "It is where the Kinga brought people for judgment. Men accused of thievery or women of adultery were pushed over the edge. If they were innocent, they would plummet to the bottom and surely perish, either on the rocks or in the river below. But if they managed to catch themselves on one of the trees on their way down, they were deemed guilty. If they climbed back up, they would be put to death for their crimes. Otherwise, they were left to fend for themselves. In which case, they would die anyway."

"How long ago was that?" someone asks.

"The practice was officially banned when the Lutherans arrived in the late nineteenth century," continues Professor Falres. "However, unofficially and quietly behind the scenes, it continued until the last known person was executed here in the 1950s."

I creep to the edge and peer over. The way down is wild and harsh, interfused with razor-sharp protrusions that would slice effortlessly through flesh. I'd hope for a quick fall, headfirst, cracking my skull on the way down, losing consciousness, tumbling bone over bone, finally splashing into aquatic cold where my benumbed body would be borne by rapids to its watery grave. Falres's voice pulls me back.

"Now we will go on to see the oldest building left here by early Lutheran missionaries, the old cathedral." He turned and pulled back the branches of one of the small trees and revealed an easy pathway through a cleft in the mountain. A dozen steps further up and we found ourselves in a small forest clearing. Several small buildings surrounded a little white clapboard building. "One of the most famous landmarks in the area…"

I stood with the rest, nodding and smiling, but only on the outside. Inside, every neuron and every muscle were screaming, "You made us struggle up a terrifying, death-defying track, leaving life and limb in limbo, writhing and roiling in terror—and all along you knew there was a perfectly safe route?"

Actually, it was pretty interesting. I settled down and listened. This first little missionary station in the Southern Highlands had been established in 1891, and the missionary station we were looking at, in 1897. Pretty cool, especially when I put this into my American context. My mother was born—baptized, confirmed, and married—into Lutheranism at a Norwegian congregation in southern Minnesota, also established in 1891.

We now headed toward Bulongwa and the climax, the apex, the *denouement* of our excursion. Ask a Tanzanian here about Bulongwa and they'll likely call it the "top of the world." Of course, there's

Kilimanjaro, which everyone knows about. But Kilimanjaro, with its fame and overcommercialization, belongs more to the world; you can't own something everyone else tracks through. Tanzanians *own* Bulongwa. It's high—964 meters above sea level. It's windy—13 knots when we arrived. Later in the year, it would be cold, even snowy, but now only pleasantly cool. The health sciences institute and hospital here are run by the Lutheran Church. We had been carefully briefed about their specialized work in dentistry and midwifery. Touring these facilities would complete our medical picture of the entire Mbeya Region. We were ushered down a hallway and led into a patient reception area and told to wait.

We waited.

It became apparent after an hour or so that they were less prepared for us than we'd expected. There were no presentations; no one took us on a services tour. No one came at all. We simply waited. Our *denouement* was slipping away.

I didn't care. For me, exhaustion, both physical and mental, had set in. Body and brain were close to shut down. We'd been told lodging would be in the Lutheran Center on the hospital grounds, and that's all I cared about. The group spread itself around the small waiting room, filling the few available chairs or lounging on the floor. I slumped down on cold tiles, back against the wall. Daylight faded, and my energy with it. Finally, well after dusk, someone rescued us. I suspect our appearance had been a surprise, that communications had broken down somewhere along the way, and that meals and beds were being prepared even as we waited.

After a restful night—good food, hot water, warm blankets, and a couple of hastily prepared requisite lectures—we divided ourselves into two groups. Our next stop would be the beautiful Metema Beach recreation area along the northern shore of Lake Nyasa. Half the group opted to do the trip on foot, a ten-mile hike down the mountain. The other half would take a longer route, making a diversionary loop through the Kitulo Plateau and around through Tukuyu. Either way would be an adventure, but I chose the one less physically arduous. I thought.

Those of us choosing to ride piled in. I waved goodbye to Russ and Karen and wished them luck. Dani, our driver, had decided to join the hikers; Sally enthusiastically jumped behind the wheel. Falres climbed in beside her, taking shotgun, and I clambered into the back. Sally is both intrepid and impetuous in personality, qualities that transfer to her driving style as well. In another lifetime, she could have driven Nascar; she's skillful and fearless. Paul had also chosen to hike, and now as she confidently jockeyed the SUV around from its narrow parking area with one hand, she waved the other vigorously out her window; "Bye, Paul! See you at Metema!" Back and forth, back and forth, she jostled the car ruthlessly around until its nose pointed down the mountain. We were off.

If I'd thought the drive up was perilous, nothing could have prepared me for the way down. Down is always tougher than up. Ladders, narrow staircases, rocky paths—I'm always more confident on the way up. On foot, going up gives one the illusion of control. Riding down in a car, not so much. Add to this the fact that if I'm in the passenger seat on mountainous terrain and looking over the side that falls away, I suffer panic attacks. I hyperventilate. My stomach wrenches. Pain shards sear behind my eyes. In my fear, I fall through the air...nothing holds me...the abyss awaits.

Negotiating the twenty-odd miles until we hit the Kitulo took a little over three hours. The road was full of switchbacks and hairpin turns. Whenever another vehicle approached, Sally would have to pull to the side and stop, letting it inch around us before we could continue. In places away from the sun, the rain that had fallen overnight still puddled on the pavement; from time to time, we'd hit a patch of moisture and skid. We were the second car, following close behind Benjamin in the lead. Our bumper came dangerously close to smacking into him when we slid. If we collided and caused a dual plummet, how ironic would that be, hoisted on our own petards! I died—or wished I could—many times over those three hours.

Why my irrational terror? Have I displaced other fears onto this one, distant and forgotten memories playing out in this specific fright, this dread replacing something I've forgotten? Perhaps it's indicative of a personality weakness, my reluctance to take chances or trust myself to the unknown. I know this: there's no self-diagnosing going on when fear strikes, nor is there the ability to be rational. The only thing I can do is take myself out of the situation, and when one is stuck in a car, the only way to do that is duck. And so for the better part of three hours, I slumped down, closed my eyes, and prayed.

The Kitolu Plateau, when we finally reached it, was vast and blessedly *flat*. All afternoon, we trundled over great stretches of desolation. There were mountains ever on the vista, but nothing proximate. Occasionally there were cattle fences, but we never saw the free-range cattle they were meant to protect. There was vegetation, but most of it was scrub and brush. I don't remember trees. Mostly just level emptiness, rough, uninhabited, wild, and hauntingly wonderful. The whole way, we never saw a car or a lorry or an SUV. We never saw another human being. At least, that's the way I remember it.

It was mostly flat highland, but that didn't mean the going was easy. Rains and subsequent erosion had taken frequent chunks out of the roadway. No highway crews had visited, and sometimes the road simply disappeared. Benjamin stopped frequently, Sally pulling up alongside. He'd jump down and run ahead to scout out the way around a gully or a washout. Sometimes we backtracked a mile or more to find a drivable course. Other times we'd plunge ahead, thumping and smashing our way over the bumps. I'd stretch my arms up and brace against the ceiling.

Depending on whose account of the day you listened to afterward, it was a long day and a wild ride (for two Americans) or a walk in the park (for the Tanzanians). The hours were sprinkled with sporadic, partial texts on our cell phones from Russ, Karen, and Paul. "Paul...trouble on the last stretch...my heart..." sent Sally into a frenzy. Her foot pounded the gas so hard that finally even Falres, the master of calm, cautioned her to slow down. He and I both assured her that Paul was strong as an ox and smart enough to handle crisis. No doubt the missing words were about someone else's trouble, that Paul being Paul was helping someone else out.

Then my own phone chirped for attention. Two messages were trying to come through. I read, "...Karen...badly brui...slippe..." from Russ's number and "Russ fell over the..." from Karen's. I wondered first how much use I'd be to an aching, injured roommate—

118

Karen—and second, how would I explain Russ's serious injuries—or death—to his wife Jo, scheduled to meet him in Dar es Salaam in a week.

We were in the mountains. Phone service was spotty at best. We heard nothing for several hours. As the day wore on, it became increasingly obvious that even as travelers, our divergent cultures separated us. The Tanzanians in the group were completely relaxed and completely trusting about both the success and the safety of the hikers. This is what Tanzanians are trained for. But by the time we reached more level plain and stopped for our midday meal—in midafternoon—Sally and I were quite desperate for news. No luck. Sally attempted to call Paul; I tried Russ's phone. Nothing. Falres, in his wisdom, decided we needed a little calm from above. We grabbed hands around the lunch table, and he prayed. "Father, these two women are worried about their loved ones, but we can do nothing, so please grant them calm." He was right. We enjoyed our chicken and chips.

And then Falres disappeared. Sally and I finished lunch and returned to the cars ready to resume the journey, but no Falres. Benjamin was gone too. We sat down on a cement wall beside the vehicles to wait. Sally was antsy. Emotions wore as the minutes ticked by. Fifteen minutes, half an hour... We wanted to arrive at Metema before our hikers, and lacking complete knowledge about their health and possible injuries, we were unraveling. Forty-five minutes, a full hour... We were worried, fraught, distressed, distracted, and frantic.

Ninety minutes. Falres and Benjamin appeared from around the corner, grinning. They each carried a bulging bag, and they looked like the luckiest men in East Africa. "This town is famous for their oranges," announced Falres, "and they were not expensive!"

"It couldn't have taken you an hour and a half to buy oranges," Sally risked.

"We also got our shoes shined," they said, pointing to four very newly burnished feet.

Finally, we were off. Sally wanted to arrive at Metema before darkness made the difficult driving even worse. Unknown roads could be impossible in the dark. Without street lighting, potholes and shadows would look equally dangerous, equally safe. And so we raced, and the quarreling continued. Oranges were one thing, but professional shoeshines quite another. To us it felt like time wasted, ego exploitation, and pridefulness. They, on the other hand, were thinking, why not? *We* knew that our Americans were out of their league on these mountains, and we were fearful of the consequences. *They* felt completely relaxed, confident their hikers were safe and having fun. This was a walk in *their* park. They didn't care about arrival time, either, because they knew that no matter what time of night we arrived, the Metema Beach Lutheran Center would have a tasty buffet laid out, fresh, hot, and delectable. In retrospect, I'm quite sure the tables would turn if, for instance, our Tanzanian hikers had been taken to a New England ski resort. In that case, we'd be comfortable; they'd be thinking they'd die. Worry made us cross.

By late afternoon, we'd left the mountains. Without warning, we'd exchanged contoured fields for jungles. Since leaving Iringa, we'd been swathed in forestry, in great stands of mountain timber waiting for logging. This was different. We'd leveled into flatness. What looked to me like California eucalyptus was draped with vines, and birds were everywhere. Great dark hawks swooped our car. Tiny brown wrens darted past if we slowed. Birdsong enveloped us. Melodic avian piping and the drone of insects: Sally turned on the windshield wipers.

Villages hidden in the tangle raced by. Pedestrians along our route barely had time to wave before we were gone. Oddly, the road here was good, the best of the day, smoothly paved as if it were newly done, which it probably was, and Sally flew.

Then suddenly there was water everywhere, standing in fields, channeling under the highway. We'd entered rice country. In one single day, from cold, foggy, rainy mountain to jungle to rice paddies!

It was a day of contrasts, not only in scenery but in emotion, from anger to wonder to fear to joy to worshipful awe—my over-stimulated brain checked out. We were all tired. Arguing and cross words were replaced with silence. Our phones were silent too with no new texts from our hikers. I was lulled to sleep. Falres was lulled to sleep. At a jolt in the road, I caught myself drooling, wondered if I had been snoring, changed position, and returned to drowsing. Falres's chin fell to his chest; he exhaled in soft little rumbles. Sally simply flew.

After a long straightaway, the car slowed, angled through a couple complex turns, and I awoke. We were passing through and under ubiquitous iron gates. A sign declared Metema Beach View, and there it was in front of us: Lake Nyasa. Behind us in the distance, the mountains; on either side, more mountains. Before us, wide white sands and deep-blue water as far as the eye could see.

Our timing was perfect; the sun was just now setting. Brilliant orange streaked the western range. Falres trotted off to secure our registrations; the rest of us turned our energies to unpacking. Grace, Professor Michael, Scola, and Atu all came running to help. They'd arrived from their mountain trek hours earlier. They looked fresh and energized. Michael was grinning out from under his fedora as usual, as if he'd just finished kicking back with students. "*Karibu*! Welcome! How was your drive?" he laughed his greeting and grabbed for the heaviest of the luggage. Atu, Grace, and Scola crowded in for hugs. I smelled cinnamon and oranges; they were fresh from showering. "We are already here long enough to have moved into our room," they said. They pointed toward a line of thatched-roof cottages peppering the beach.

"No sign of Russ or Karen? Paul?" we asked. "Are they hurt? Have they fallen?" We began peppering them with questions.

"Who broke a bone? Which bones?"

"What about the injuries? Cuts? Bruises?"

"What about Paul? Did you see him on the mountain? Was he struggling? Why did you leave him there? You should have stayed to help him!"

"Should we call the authorities? Do you think he's lost? Are they all lost?"

They assured us all was well. The Americans, they said, were merely very slow because they were "unacquainted with mountain routes."

"But Paul," said Sally. "He said something about his heart. I thought he was having a heart attack."

"And Karen," I added. "Russ texted that she was hurt."

We explained about the phone texts, how they came through only partially because of poor reception. Sally and I opened our phones to show them. They read through everything and laughed some more. Karen, they said, had fallen and skinned her knees. But otherwise, they were all fine. "Only slow. Very, very slow."

We heard a shout—or at least the attempt of a shout. It was more like a whimper trying to be a shout. The first of the very, very slow emerged from a narrow path leading out from the trees. It was Russ, bedraggled but erect, tired but smiling, surrounded with a quiet glow of accomplishment.

Next came Paul. Sally ran toward him and caught him in an embrace. "Paul, I was so worried! I thought you'd had a heart attack!"

"No, my dear heart. I'm just fine. Only tired."

And so we spent two days on Metema Beach. On the first, absolutely nothing happened. Unless one calls lying on soft white sand, taking quick but luxurious dips in clear deep waters, being forced to eat three gourmet meals, and chatting and singing around a beach fire in the evening "something." Heaven. I felt as if I were at an expensive resort. The catch? Everything was prepaid and so cheap it was a bit insane. Our thatched-roof beach cottages had comfortable beds, maid service with turndowns, complete baths, electric lights until 8:00 p.m., and thereafter a hurricane lamp lit by house servants. What wasn't to love?

The second day we met Harrison Mwakembe, member of Parliament, senior lecturer of law at the University of Dar, current Minister of Transportation, and an honest man. It's the honesty part that continually gets him in trouble in this country. He goes so far as to expect fellow politicians to be trustworthy, and they don't always concur. At least once it's gotten him poisoned. On that occasion, all the members of the Lutheran congregation where he worships moved into the church sanctuary, living communally and praying for several days until he recovered. Continued threats to his safety and that of his family make his life challenging. Still, more folks respect him than not. Some even hope he'll one day consider himself a candidate for the presidency.

He invited us to lunch at a fancy restaurant. Mwakembe inspires admiration, even awe, when he speaks. You immediately feel his authority. We listened as he outlined some of the biggest problems facing the people of his district. He knows his stuff. He also knows his audience. Recognizing us as educators from two contrasting worlds, he drew us into discussion about breaking down barriers between systems, finding consistencies and compromise, and then being able to apply the same to break down barriers between economic groups, between the rich and the poor, because, really, all the problems in the world ultimately stem from one dichotomy: the haves versus the have-nots. The complex made simple.

We left the restaurant inspired. Mwakembe saw us to our vehicles, shook hands all around, promised to stay in touch, and wished us Godspeed. He'd both inspired and challenged us. We felt ready to take on the world. Challenged, valuable, of use, perhaps even a bit infatuated with our power, we piled in, waving now and shouting farewells. The restaurant guards pulled back the iron gates to let our Land Rovers through. Mwakembe and the restaurant staff lined the driveway, as if at attention for these important educators who were about to save the world.

Our car wouldn't start.

Dani clambered out, opened the hood, and tinkered. He tried again, but the engine refused to turn over. The minutes passed. He checked carburetor, spark plugs, and battery; water level and petrol. He fiddled with wires. The restaurant staff went back inside. The guard sat back in his chair and put his feet up. Mwakembe and Dani held a consultation, and Dani climbed behind the wheel. Mwakembe walked to the rear and put his shoulder to the metal, and the car rolled forward. Dani popped the clutch and the engine caught. The great man brushed the dust from his hands and waved a final goodbye.

From the restaurant, we drove straight to Mwandenga, the border crossing between Tanzania and Malawi. "Come, I will take you across." And Falres beckoned me out of the vehicle. "You can then tell everyone that you've been to Malawi. Bring your camera and take photos for proof." By this time I would have followed Falres to the moon. I followed.

He marched the five of us—the Americans—up to a group of guards at the gates and addressed them in Swahili. A spirited discussion ensued; we understood none of it but knew from tone, inflexion, and gestures that what was said was important. Two guards with machetes and AK-47s walked toward us and held out hands in greeting. They saluted. We were escorted through walls of concrete and several pair of steel gates.

This is the country dubbed "The Warm Heart of Africa." There was a bridge to walk across. Having just left the lake that separates most of Tanzania from this country, I registered idly that the river flowing beneath was probably a tributary that acted like a great natural moat for this side of the country. The bustle of city life was laid out in front of us, and mountain ranges towered beyond. Those, I registered, were the geographical evidence that I was now on the opposite side of the Great Rift Valley.

We merged ourselves into the foot traffic of the city. My camera was out, and I was snapping as rapidly as possible. I spun to take in 360 degrees of Malawi: water in two directions, mountains behind and mountains before, a "Welcome to Malawi" sign on the bridge with "Leaving Malawi for Tanzania" in the distance, crowds of people in every direction, hurrying toward their businesses. I left the security of the bridge, turned onto what looked to be a main street, and found myself in a congregate of kiosks. It felt familiar; it felt a bit like Iringa's Central Market. I dug around in my bag for my wallet, wondering if Tanzanian shillings were welcome here. And then it struck me: my wallet and my passport were in a Land Rover in Tanzania.

On returning to America, I would purchase and read Paul Theroux's novel, *The Lower River,* in which a middle-aged businessman from New England would return to Malawi to the place he'd spent his peace corps years, hoping to recapture something of his youth. What he'd find instead is that the country trapped him—physically, emotionally, and intellectually. He couldn't escape. Reading his plight, I'd be reminded of my own panic. Finding oneself in Malawi without a passport must surely be the ultimate *mzungu* experience. It feels dangerous and vulnerable. Maybe it wasn't a big deal. If I'd been asked for my passport and ID and couldn't produce it, maybe the Malawian police force wouldn't care. But maybe they would. People have been detained for lesser reasons. It was possible for a person without a passport to suffer huge consequence that even the US Embassy would find disturbing. While I always felt like an outsider in Tanzania, at least I was legal. I had authorization from two governments, and I enjoyed protection from several directions—Tumaini, Bega Kwa Bega, and the diocese; Iringa's regional director; Cosmos, and my night guards; even Falres. Like a bolt of lightning, it occurred to me, at that moment and in that particular place, that *mzungu* means more than being foreign. It means more than being an outsider, someone who doesn't understand, someone who might not be granted acceptance. At its most extreme, it means existing somewhere without protection.

Once, in America, I stood in an airfield and watched my daughter skydive. Tethered to her guide, she shared his parachute. From that vantage, she could enjoy the wonder of weightlessness, the air rushing past, the panoramic view, the challenge to all physical, emotional, and intellectual senses and still feel secure. Being *mzungu* in Tanzania was a bit like that. My tethers (everything listed above and more) allowed me to engage my senses and explore and still feel safe. In Malawi, if caught, I was tetherless. It was possible that an official—any one of the dozens of guards with machetes, any one of the hundreds of citizens milling around me on their rightful business—could turn me in.

Obviously, that didn't happen. I didn't get arrested, didn't get thrown into jail, didn't even get asked for my passport. My excursion into Malawi was short-lived and uneventful. But as Falres said, I can tell everyone that I've been to Malawi.

By evening, we were home again in Iringa. Our night guard was glad to see us, especially after I handed him the half pizza left over from supper. I unpacked and showered, reviewed some lesson notes, and curled up with my laptop, intending to write home about our adventures. I awoke eight hours later, my laptop tangled in the sheets. I'd dreamed. A madman had approached, and several of the group surrounded me. He threatened us all. Karen took my hand for security, and Gloria said, "I'll explain it to you." Then there had been a lot of falling. Whether I'd jumped, been pushed, or lost my balance, I don't know. But I had a parachute.

Who or what is the definition of "wild"?

Is it the man on the mountain lying in wait for the errant tourist who might need direction? He knew by our appearance that we had the means to reward his efforts monetarily. Granted we didn't respond in the way he'd expected, but was that his fault? Perhaps he'd approached us in a manner acceptable in his culture. I had been quick to assess his mental state and assume the sort of treatment he should receive, but who am I to say there are limited ways to handle mental instability? Maybe the whole incident was our fault. We didn't understand his language. If we'd understood his words, maybe we'd have been grateful enough to reward him. After all, he knew we had the means.

Is it the midwife bending beside her fire to bury a fresh placenta, buried to guarantee fertility for the mother suckling her newborn? The words of imprecation...fragrant wood smoke fanned beneath the nostrils of a newborn reluctant to take her first breath...crushed herbs gently packed around the new mother's bloody vagina...the almost total absence (sterile razor blades the only exception) of clinical intervention. And yet most of her babies live.

Could it be the Kinga tribal court flinging their prisoner over the ledge? He's broken their laws and breached their covenants, rupturing the social fabric. He should be punished. Perhaps it's the arbitrary nature of the punishment (guilty if he plunges, innocent but still doomed if he doesn't) that bothers us. But who's to say this judicial system is any more unfair or arbitrary than ours. We're sometimes guilty of imposing penalties too severe for the crime, decades behind bars for minor drug dealing, for instance. We change our minds about what's legal and what isn't—alcohol, abortion, homosexuality—but there's little justice in hindsight when we change the rules. And sometimes, we flat out get it wrong and condemn the innocent.

I no longer felt so sure of my own mores and my own culture.

Was I now better off for what I'd witnessed or not? In five days, for $55, I'd seen and experienced things most Americans never will. I had learned much. I needed to figure out how to apply knowledge to action, how to fit this stuff into my life.

How, for instance, would it affect my teaching for the remainder of this semester? What now would my students think of me? Many of them had never had the chance to travel like that. For most, $55 United States will always be prohibitive. If they couldn't afford the Mkwawa Museum—which cost pennies—they surely couldn't have afforded a five-day faculty tour. (I learned later that the two students who accompanied us went gratis, their fees picked up by the university.) Money wasn't the only prohibiting factor. Could Edgar or Given, both of whom had full-time jobs and family responsibilities beyond their student roles, have taken off the time?

However I was changed, and however I managed to convey what had changed me, I would have to learn to tell the story—my story—without prejudice, without pride, and without haughtiness. At stake is my personal ethos and my values. My words can never demean my African friends. It boils down to this: respect for their culture and acknowledgment for my own. Had I not seen theirs, I would not have been forced to examine mine. Seeing theirs forces me to interrogate mine, to ask what's good, what's not so good; what can be approved, what needs to be overhauled.

Indeed, I would be staring into the fire for a long, long time.

11

Sounds, Smells, Rain

I wake to the sound of rain on the roof, to the knowledge of another dark and dreary morning. This is the rainy season. Folks here name periods by the weather rather than by our four orbitally determined seasons. They have both short and long rainy seasons, and we're in the middle of the long one. The windy season will arrive in a couple of weeks. Since early April, morning after morning, I've awakened to rain. Sometimes thunder rumbles in the distance. By midday, skies will clear and sunshine return, conveniently just in time for an afternoon shopping amble.

Of course, the rain is welcome. This area of the Iringa District is richly agricultural, the "bread basket of Tanzania." Farmers love the rain as it determines the success of their crops. Cosmos loves it; our yard is becoming a spectacle of color. Between regular morning rain and afternoon sun, his plots proliferate—roses, poinsettia, gardenia, lilies, azaleas, lupines, gladiola, hibiscus, hollyhocks, and sunflowers. Each day, we find him puttering around with arcane techniques and secret solutions. One of his tricks is to burn our food scraps and turn the ashes into fertilizer. He also has something magic he cooks up from fruit rinds to keep bugs away. He's turning our digs into Eden.

Cosmos is a rather lackadaisical guard, abandoning his post during the day if he thinks we'll be away, performing a sleight of hand with a stick in the gate lock so that it appears secure—at least for the sixty seconds it takes us to figure it out. And he has a habit of shortening his days, arriving late, leaving early, always with a good excuse. His son is ill. His aging mother-in-law needs him. He has to sit with a sick friend. My favorite: he has to "spend the day in prayer." But for all his weakness as guard, he's a crackerjack gardener. Is it coincidence that "lackadaisical" has a flower in its middle? Turns out he'd apprenticed with a horticulturist in an earlier situation. What that man can do with a hoe and a water hose is pure wizardry. When I tell him that in English, "cosmos" is also the name of a flower, he's completely delighted. "Is that true?" he asks. "Wait!" He runs into his shack. He comes out wearing his suitcoat, a clean but shabby number that doubles as his outer jacket because he has no other. He strikes a pose against a banana tree. "I am Cosmos, the master gardener, the sweetest smelling flower!"

Back to the rain. Often it comes in deluge, and then it leaks into everything. It seeps through window frames and puddles across our floors. It does a number on the roads. Along Iringa's streets are deep ditches—gullies—designed as protection from the torrent. When they overflow, roads wash away. Making our way around town in the long rainy season can be a challenge.

About those gullies: When a wandering elephant fell into one, Iringa's police had to bring in heavy equipment from Dar es Salaam to lift him out. A woman visiting from Minneapolis stepped off her tour bus, fell into one, broke her leg, and had to be sent home to Minnesota the next day. I stumbled into one on a dark night when I'd forgotten my flashlight and scraped up my hand, wrist, and arm pretty badly. Poor Russ had to do surgery with a tweezers and manicure scissors to dig out all the gravel.

A particular irony is that when it rains too much too fast, our taps no longer deliver water. That's because the gullies also collect debris. Debris clogs the sewers, the delivery pipes back up, and the whole system stops. Each time it happens, Cosmos negotiates with the guard at the Hilltop next door for buckets of water.

We're home from our faculty tour not more than a couple of days when Sally calls. "I won't be coming to campus tomorrow," she tells me. "Falres is in jail."

Falres had been driving in the countryside near Iringa, checking on research he was doing for a new book. Just as he approached his target village, a small child ran out in front of his car. It happened in an instant. One moment he was driving down an empty road; the next, a child hit his windshield.

The little girl probably died instantly, her mother and baby brother watching from the side. Falres scooped up the small broken body, urged mother and baby into his car, and drove straight to the village police station to fill out the requisite reports. It was the mother who remonstrated against the police filing that would put the driver under arrest. "It was my child's own fault," she kept crying. But in Tanzanian law, blame is apportioned. So Falres went to jail.

Falres's accident and incarceration were routine enough not to make the newspapers, but a second accident that week appeared on the front page. Harrison Mwakembe, member of Parliament, whistle-blower on government embezzlement, was en route between Mbeya District and Iringa District, driving through the mountains, when his car went over the side. A second sooner or later, a dozen meters more or less, and it would have plunged a hundred feet to the river below, but it hit a tree. Mwakembe survived; his driver was killed.

An ambulance took Mwakembe to Iringa Hospital to await a helicopter, and then he was flown to a medical facility in Dar es Salaam. In the newspaper account, a reporter claimed that from his hospital bed, Mwakembe described how there had been two other vehicles on the road with them, one in front, one following, and that they had colluded to force his car over the side. It seems plausible. I've been on that road, and I know how easily one could go over. Put that knowledge together with earlier attempts made on his life, and the account is believable.

Within a few weeks, Mwakembe made a full recovery and was back to work. Falres was released on bail and given permission to return to normal work while awaiting trial.

All the while, it just kept raining. On my part, there was heaviness. I felt like I was slogging the remaining days and weeks now, realizing that systems were unfair, realizing how long it takes for things to change, realizing that things might not improve in time for my new friends to reap the benefits. Maybe it was partially the weather, but I was at an emotional low. The whole thing with Falres shouldn't have happened in so many ways to a man like him: as a law-abiding citizen, as a humanitarian, as a professor, as a parent, a scholar, and an ethically caring man. It happens everywhere that there's unfairness, but now it seemed more often so in Tanzania. And yet Falres wasn't rebelling against the system in the way I wanted to. I was angry. There was something in his understanding that was different from mine.

Part of the explanation might be that as a US citizen, I was both raised and educated to think I'm partly responsible for my government and its actions. In Tanzania, I often hear people say, "Yes, there's corruption…violence…lack of concern for individuals from the government. But…" Then they go on about their business. In my experience, at least among my friends and colleagues, professional people in America tend to be politically aware, and awareness leads to activism. Here, the college professors, religious leaders, attorneys, businessmen, all sorts of civic-minded folks I've met might well complain about the legal or political systems they live under, but then, knowing they can't do much about it, are able to shrug their shoulders and get on with things. I find myself wishing I could do the same. On a personal level, when I'm overseas, I always feel a bit responsible for my government. I feel I'm representing American political views, especially as they impact world matters. Not so, my Tanzanian friends.

I saw this ambivalence toward unfairness play out in a minor way on our faculty tour. At one juncture, in an audience with a woman who'd been newly appointed District Minister of Tourism, we were asked for our opinions about the area. It was late afternoon, we hadn't eaten since breakfast, we'd been detained on impassable mountain roads for four hours, and we'd arrived expecting a buffet lunch only to be told, "So sorry, you're too late. *Pole!*" Now we'd listened for close to an hour as she droned on about her innovations and improvements, handing around her commission's newest brochures and lists of presentations. "So now, tell me what you think. How do you find all this? Pleasant?" We looked down, avoiding her gaze, and fidgeted in our seats until Gloria, brave Gloria the tourism major, brought up the impassable roads: "If you want tourists to come, you must provide a way for them to get here."

Without missing a beat, the official replied, "Yes, of course, we know the roads are bad and that no one will come. But how are we doing with tourism?" It's not ignorance. It's not denial. It's not exactly blind acceptance either. It's more like, "Yes—it's bad, we know that, but we can't do anything about it. What's next?"

Maybe it's fatalism.

Maybe it's faith. The system, after all, did eventually find Falres innocent, although it would take a whole year of uncertainty before that would happen. In the meantime, he was supported by his faith community. They prayed and prayed, and just as Mwakembe had found support, Falres and his family were encouraged. Prayer found the money to pay his legal fees; prayer took care of his family while he was away. Falres would be the first to tell you that prayer secured his freedom.

I think about the way Falres began his life, born on the mountainside between medicinal fires, a midwife pulling him from his mother's womb, ready with incense to soothe, aloes to cleanse, and magic words to pray over him. In our sterile American hospitals, we think we know better, and we're a bit nonplussed to think babies in other parts of the world are born without modern science. Our systems are superior, we claim. But then Falres—the man of modern science—says, "I lived," and that's proof enough for him. Faith. Fatalism. Sure, maybe someone's system is broken. Perhaps all our systems are a bit broken. We know it. We move on. It matters; it doesn't matter.

And suddenly, it's the windy season. One day it rains heavily, the next day it simply doesn't. No in between, nothing gradual. Falres was back at work at the university as if things were normal. Mwakembe had recovered, returned home, and resumed political service.

I lie in my bed at night in awe. Now instead of thunder, I hear the work of the wind. It makes the air whine through the stones in our wall wherever the cement has crumbled. Cement pellets fly up against my windows. The iron gate outside rattles and whistles. Some nights I hear objects flying around—branches, a lost sheaf of papers, an occasional sheet of plywood. The dogs guarding our neighbors' livestock bay with agitation, and mountain baboons yip back with ghostly squeals. Some nights the sounds over my head—seed pods pelting the corrugated roof—make sleep elusive.

The night temperature is beginning to drop now; winter is approaching. I huddle under extra blankets, cocooned beneath mosquito netting. Our windows fit so poorly that even when they're cranked shut, the cold seeps through. Why did I not think to pack flannel pj's? I compensate with a sweatshirt.

How wild this must all seem to our night guards as they shiver in their miserable little shack. One of them—the skinny guy with a perpetual plastic spoon (?) hanging from his mouth—takes regular refuge on our front porch. There's a battered old folding chair the guards drag around the yard, and around midnight I'll hear it scraping the porch wall. He sits there beneath my window, coughing and coughing. I don't think he's well, and night guarding is definitely not a job for the infirm.

As I lie awake, listening, I ponder again the meaning of wild. Who or what is wild? To be wild is to be feral, but it's also to be natural and unfettered. Surely the Kinga lifestyle Falres had shown us in his mountains was closer to being natural than my complicated modern American ways. When I consider the systematic layers of responsibility under and inside of which I live back home—family, church, social clubs, university loyalties, professional work, teaching—let alone the constant pressures, I place on myself for personal improvement—practicing my arts, increasing my professional knowledge base, keeping abreast of electronic developments, staying politically aware (the lists go on and on…), the weight is substantial. Add on exercising regularly, eating healthy, and staying enough in fashion so as not to embarrass my kids. By those definitions, I'm the wild one. I'm overwhelmed; I'm *fettered*.

12

Guards and Guarding

"It is not safe, Big Sister. A woman should not walk alone."

By this time, Cosmos and I had exchanged enough personal information that our relationship had grown beyond business to friendship. Curious about my family, he'd asked about my parents and siblings. I told him, even including a story about my younger brother who'd been killed in an accident. "Did he have a good life?" he'd asked. "When was he born?" and I told him. "Ah, the same year as me. You miss him. Then I will be your little brother." Since then, he often called me Big Sister.

"Cosmos, I'll be fine. It's bright daylight. I'll stick to the main roads and the market. People know me."

"It is not proper. I will follow." With that assertion, Cosmos slammed the gate shut, threaded a stick through the lock so he could let himself back in, and took his place two steps behind me.

"I'm not paying any attention to you, Cosmos. Go back. I'm fine alone." A few steps later, he muttered his discontent, turned, and left me on my own.

I loved heading out into our neighborhood on foot. I'd grab camera, phone, and a shopping basket and wend my way down the hill, snapping flowers, lizards, soccer-playing kids, ivied iron gates, and rock formations. Cosmos was wary about my being alone. I wasn't. Truth was, I was never really alone. No matter where I went, there would be a student watching or a street vendor or another neighborhood guard reporting my location back to Cosmos.

Guarding is the next largest profession in Tanzania, second only to farming. Every upper-class household and every business employ guards, one for day, another for night. Most business guards are armed with a rifle, though I always wonder how many of those are actually loaded. Some employ an entire force, especially when the commodity dealt is expensive or highly desired, as at our favorite petrol station. Two of them stood sentinel there, AK-47s trained straight at us as we'd drive in. "Hey, Professors!" they'd shout. "You fine today? You welcome!" all the while smiling and nodding behind their rifles.

The guard at the Hilltop carried a rifle too. Since Russ and I always frequented the *bandas* late afternoon or early evening, we only ever saw one guard, weekdays or weekends. "We be cope!" he informed us early on as he nodded toward Wilolesi and Cosmos. We took it to be a declaration of cooperation between guards. "Cope" was stunningly jaunty, red beret pulled menacingly down his forehead, his rifle slung over his shoulder and dangling down his back like a lady's handbag. Hilltop buildings marched up the hill in sequence; Cope marched up in sync. The vast complex had a single driveway entrance from which its line of buildings followed a stone ledge on one side, a taller stone wall opposite. Cope would emerge from the upper reaches precisely the moment we'd be seating ourselves (I think he watched for our arrival), wave his rifle, grin, and salute. Then he'd disappear from view. Fifteen minutes later, he'd emerge again from the top of his circuit and repeat: wave, grin, salute.

Back from my wanderings one late afternoon, I stood at the gate, banged a moment, and called for Cosmos to let me in. He came running. "Sister, see what I've found!" He held out his hand to show me an American dime.

He asked the value, and I translated it into T-shillings. It would buy enough beans at the Central Market for a family meal. He asked what it would buy in America, and all I could come up with was penny candy from a vending machine. When I told him to keep it, he was delighted. "Wait a minute…" I went inside to find other American coins, a penny, a nickel, and a quarter.

The quarter intrigued him. This one featured Alaska. I explained that we'd issued a whole series, one for each state. He rolled it in his hand. We discussed the bear for a bit, intriguing since there are no bears in Tanzania. "Now I know about bears in America," he grinned. "In Alaska." He held the coin up and punctuated his knowledge with a head bob.

"Yes, Alaska," I said. "Do you know where that is?"

He gave me one of his sly grins. "Alaska...no, but you can see Russia from there!" And then he slapped his knee and giggled delightedly at his cleverness.

Clever he was. Somehow this man who lived in a tiny hovel at the foot of the Udzugwa Mountains outside Iringa, Tanzania, a place with no electricity, no internet—no NPR, CNN, or the *New York Times*—knew enough about American political talk to spot the silliness in a candidate's supposed claim of "seeing Russia" from her back deck in Juneau.

Which begs the question: How? It wasn't the first time this man I'd become proud to call friend, this man full of contradictions, surprised me. This was the person who once asked me about the advisability of America's bicameral congress when the two bodies spent most of their time disagreeing, who told me that a two-party political system limited possibility, but who then declared that Tanzania should throw out its antiquated government and copy the US system. Once he outlined the US railway system for me. When and where was such information acquired? His English, his degree of world knowledge, hinted at education way beyond his position of guard. Perhaps I'll never fully understand the mystery that is Cosmos.

A few days after the Alaska incident, I was again out in the yard. Cosmos was picking beans from the vegetable patch. He offered me a hatful.

"Sister, I have a question," he began. "Father...[one of his names for Russ]...Professor...[the other name] is not your husband, is he?" I could see where this was leading. Russ was away—the Serengeti, the Ngorogoro Crater, Kilimanjaro—with his wife Jo who'd flown in to meet him. I was at Wilolesi alone. Cosmos had always been curious about our relationship; present circumstances were even more confusing. Had I been jilted? In Tanzanian society, open friendship between the sexes is not the norm. And living under the same roof! In the beginning he'd thought I was Russ's secretary. The day he discovered that I too was teaching at Tumaini... "You a professor?" he positively hooted. He acted as if it was the most ridiculous and outrageous thing he'd ever heard.

"Sister, do you have a husband?" he asked now.

"Just a minute," I said. "I'll show you." I went inside and fetched my laptop, pulling up a photo of Kurt.

We sat down on the rocks, and I scrolled through a series of family photos. "My three daughters," I narrated, "two grandchildren, Noah is seven and Merete is six...my youngest daughter with her husband...the whole family together at Christmas...here's my house..."

"You *have* a husband. What is his name?" I scrolled back to Kurt's picture. Cosmos touched the screen. "He looks very respectable," he pronounced. With that he nodded, picked up his hoe, and turned back to his work. I flipped the laptop closed and started back to the house.

Halfway, I felt a tap on my shoulder. "But how did he get inside that machine?"

Then there was the day when I climbed behind the wheel of the van: "You drive a car?" I pulled out my international license and showed him. "Ah, very respectable."

Besides Cosmos, Wilolesi had night guards and Sunday guards, all provided by Tumaini. They knew our every move and sound and smell. Excepting Cosmos, we knew almost nothing about the rest, not even their names. One we called "Soap" after we made the discovery about his bathing at our outdoor tap. Elia we knew because he introduced himself anew each time he arrived: "Elia here" as he tapped his chest. Others became familiar because during the day, they hung out at the university guardhouse, calling greetings when they saw our van approaching, quickly dragging back the gate so we wouldn't have to slow down as we drove onto campus. Tumaini's front gate was constant activity with vehicles and foot traffic. There were always guys hanging out, joking, playing cards, trading smokes.

Plus there were university facilities—cafeteria, convenience store—within reach. Not so at Wilolesi. One night, I offered Elia the box of leftover pizza after Russ's and my supper downtown. He grinned broadly and woofed it down; obviously, he hadn't had supper before coming on duty. Thereafter, all our leftovers found their way to the guard shack.

That guard shack was pretty bad: four foot square, dirt floor, no light or heat save what blew in between the boards. Shoved up against the back was a narrow cot with a dirty blanket. No bathroom facilities. Those processes were affected between the tool shed at the rear of the property and the stone retaining wall. Wilolesi boasted three bathrooms, but a guard wouldn't come into the house unless there was an emergency, and that would have to be an emergency greater than pee. The interior of the house where the university professors lived was off-limits.

To illustrate how serious the guards took this injunction, "Ellen" told us her story. Ellen was an eighty-year-old retired social worker from the States who'd taught for a semester a couple of years before we arrived and who had been housed at Wilolesi. One morning, alone in the house, she slipped in the shower in the very bathroom I now occupied, lodging herself on the floor between the shower surround and the toilet. It was the hard, fast fall of a slippery nude body onto unforgiving ceramic tiles. She was knocked out. When she regained consciousness, a terrific pain told her she'd broken a couple of ribs. Movement was impossible. Her cell phone was on the bed; she could see it but couldn't reach it. She was cold and couldn't cover herself. She needed to summon help, so she used the only thing left: her voice. As loudly as able she screamed, hoping the guard would hear and rescue her. Indeed, he heard. Except in lieu of entering the house, he went for help, walking four kilometers to the university, which then summoned a vehicle to take her to the hospital.

But one day when we were away teaching, Pia, the woman who came weekly to clean and do laundry, had an emergency great enough for Cosmos to venture inside. Pia was scrubbing the toilet in my bathroom when it sprung a leak. Actually, it sprung a flood. The connecting pipe between water tank and bowl burst open, sending the tank's contents across the bathroom and into the bedroom. She called Cosmos, and Cosmos, ever willing to reinvent himself, now became plumber. When we returned home several hours later, he handed us his pencil diagram of the problem and urged us to go in and investigate. He'd taken a plastic shopping bag, wrapped it around the broken pipe, and taped the whole thing together with masking tape (where did *that* come from?) "It works fine now for a long time," he said with pride.

Cosmos was reliable. The night guards were another matter. One night, returning around nine after supper with Beau, a Bega Kwa Bega friend, we found our guard unresponsive. I knocked and called repeatedly, but with no answer. Remembering Cosmos's trick with the stick, I fumbled at the lock. It didn't budge. Beau banged the metal and shouted, but no guard appeared. "Some guard," he said. "Some security system. We'll see about this." And with that, Beau jumped up, grabbed the top of the wall, hoisted a leg over, and plopped himself on the opposite side of our eight-foot fortification. He found our guard sound asleep in the shack—probably stoned— but when Beau hauled him out, he stood cockily at attention and declared his readiness. Tumaini fired him the next day.

So our fortress wasn't impenetrable. Our neighborhood had begun as one of two privileged enclaves for white settlers, Wilolesi in Iringa's western foothills, Mkwawa across the way to the east. Perhaps when first built, the wall surrounding our property was strong, even formidable, but time and disrepair had taken their tolls. Some places were badly deteriorated, chipping away to powder. The metal gates looked fierce, but they hung loosely on their hinges, scraping the ground, screaming their pain every time they were dragged open. The guard shack was nothing but a crumble. Everything, we knew, was for appearance, even the unarmed guards.

On our level and above, all the homes were stonewalled, and most looked stronger. We were on the line of demarcation. The homes below us had rusting corrugated steel for protection or fabricated wood panels. Or dogs.

What determined the line of demarcation seemed to be whatever possessions the occupants had to protect. The homes on our level—by all appearances—were those of people with wealth. Russ and I had brought along very little in the way of value. I had a computer, but that was our only electronic device. We had no cash to speak of; no jewelry, no collectables, no expensive wardrobes. Other homes, however, bespoke comfort, if not actual wealth, especially by Iringa standards. Below us, things were decidedly different. No residence there had a guard. The yards were full of chickens, goats, a few cows, and lots of kids. Hence, dogs. These weren't show dogs; no poodles, no Pomeranians, no shih tzus. These were hounds, large and brown, but of undeterminable breed. Just dogs. In fact, I asked a neighbor one day when I saw her putting food out for the dog what breed he was, and she said, "I dunno. Brown, I guess."

Cosmos hated dogs. He'd throw stones at any that dared come near Wilolesi, and he whacked at least one with his hoe.

Our last full day arrived. Russ and I emptied cupboards and packed our suitcases. There was much that we didn't want and no longer needed: canned food, bottles of aspirin and boxes of bandages, empty notebooks and a hole punch, towels, soap, hairspray, and T-shirts. There were the items I'd insisted we buy from Mbata to decorate the house: sofa pillows, baskets, carvings…and a wall map of Tanzania. We loaded all of it into the van and called Cosmos.

"Get your bicycle and come," said Russ. "Show us the way to your house." Russ threw the bike into the back and held the side door open.

The grin on Cosmos's face at being offered a ride in the van! I caught it and grabbed his arm before he could climb in. "No, no, take the front seat. I'll climb in the back," I said and maneuvered in around him before he could protest. After all the hours, soap, and precious water he'd expended on washing our vehicle, no doubt all the while thinking it was the closest he'd get to ownership, sitting in the front seemed appropriate.

We drove to the edge of town and down the escarpment, the same escarpment Cosmos cycled up every morning and down every night. At the bottom, we turned onto the road toward the villages and then onto a dirt sidetrack. Russ slowed the van, and I could tell he was carefully negotiating ruts and furrows, avoiding sharp rocks that could puncture a tire. Fifteen slow kilometers later, we pulled up in front of a cluster of mud huts. A small crowd gathered as Russ stopped the van. Cosmos opened the door and nonchalantly stepped down, enjoying a moment of importance. "That's my home," he said, pointing to a hut in the center.

A woman stood in the doorway. Cosmos barked a command, and she ducked back inside, returning with four boys in tow. She lined them up. "These are my sons!" beamed Cosmos. "Joshua, who will soon be in university, Andrew in Form Four, Daniel and James in elementary school. They all speak excellent English! Talk to them and you will see." We exchanged greetings and shook hands all around. There was a flurry of the usual small talk between us and the four boys. Stella, his wife, hung quietly in the background but offered her hand and curtsied when I came toward her.

Cosmos pushed her toward me. "You may talk women things," he said, but then changed his mind as he thought of something else. Turning his attention to Stella, he asked, "We have another child, don't we?"

Very quietly, she answered, "Yes. Restuta. The girl."

No wonder he was surprised that a woman would be a university professor.

It is a great sadness of my life that, barring a miracle, I will not see Cosmos again. There's no way for me to contact him; he has no phone, no e-mail address, no mailing address. As close as we eventually became, I don't even know his last name. He'll forever be lodged in my memory, his kindness and caring nature, his humor, his earnest "Jesus Christ in my heart" that preceded every request. Banging his fist on his chest, he'd declare "Jesus Christ in my heart, I need a hoe...my bicycle fixed...tuition for my son's school." He always approached me first, perhaps because he expected me to be the easier mark, but every time, I deferred financial negotiations to Russ. I'd step aside, hang back, look Cosmos sheepishly in the eye, and shrug. Inevitably Russ became the bad guy and I the sympathizer.

He taught me much. A universal truth about knowledge is that the more you learn, the more questions you develop. Certainly knowing Cosmos did that for me. I think I taught him things as well.

I enlarged his picture of womanhood, although it may well be that what I represented is something he interpreted as belonging only to white American women, not extending far enough to include Stella or Restuta.

In these ways, Cosmos represents much of what I learned in Africa—contradictions.

The irony is that while we can identify contradictions in other societies, it's often impossible to see them in our own.

13

Animal Friends

Grass rustling, soft snorting, the chuff-chuff sound of delicate hooves. The time, 2:00 a.m., glows from the desk clock across the room. I sit up in bed to listen, and through the dim light, I see Kurt stirring beside me. My eyes plead a silent question: Does he hear what I hear? He nods.

We've been sound asleep, tired out by the day's activities. First, a mind-numbing four-hour drive over rutted roads between Iringa and the Ruaha National Park. Then registration at Mwagusi Safari Camp, check-in, lunch, and our first exhilarating, sometimes white-knuckled, ride in a Land Rover around the park—animals up close, nose-to-nose, intimate, terrifying, and wonderful. Supper on the dry riverbed under the stars was magnificent—campfire, white linens and jacketed waiters, fine wine in silver coolers, candles glowing from the banks—but exhausting. Finally we'd been escorted back to our quarters for the night, trundling through loose sand, following our guide's swinging lamp. Rounding the last corner and reaching our *banda*, we stepped up to our hammock-ed veranda from where we'd be watching river action along the Mwagusi the next morning, slipped through the canvas tent flap, and answered, "Oh-yes-please!-two-coffees-and-an-early-wakeup-call-sounds-lovely!" Our guide zipped us safely into soft light. We found ourselves in a spacious room, king-size bed (African print quilts and chocolates on the pillows), a large writing desk, and a safari trunk in the corner, personal belongings already neatly packed inside.

My husband Kurt had flown over to spend a couple of weeks with me, and we'd come to Mwagusi with a group of friends. The bandas here are luxurious three-room tents—canvas ceilings and walls on stone foundations, elegant hot-water baths and dressing rooms. We marveled at the luxury, really too exhausted to take it all in, promising ourselves to fully appreciate it in the morning.

And now, four hours into slumber, the two of us are awakened by night sounds. The sounds are soft—more presence than noise. We're aroused by strangeness, a peculiarity in the atmosphere rather than sound itself. We hold our breath; outside, animals. I turn on my stomach and peek through the canvas window and see giraffe legs. A herd is going by, a dozen, maybe more. Mottled stilts flex with grace, supporting precarious bodies. We only see legs, but we can tell from the height of the knees that some are taller—male—and others smaller—females. A tiny head appears among the legs, a baby sheltered beneath her mother's body. In the moonlight, Kurt and I catch each other's eyes but remain silent as the chuffing continues.

Our silence is wonder, tinged perhaps with a bit of fear. After all, the territory is theirs. The camp has encroached. We are intruders, invaders.

We watch. What do they think of us? The wild places and the animals that inhabit them are dwindling, and so we humans attempt solutions. We tell ourselves that safari camps and wildlife reservations are methods of conservation, not perfect, we know, but better than doing nothing. We've evolved from tracking and poaching and killing for pleasure. We shoot now with cameras. After safari, we hang enlargements over our fireplaces in lieu of stuffed heads, and we print smaller versions for Christmas letters. We like the dramatic photos the best: a mama elephant charging to protect her calf, a leopard screaming from his perch in a baobab, a herd of zebra fleeing in terror as our Rover rips through. Simulated poaching versus actual poaching and the boundaries between are topics with which we struggle. Sadly, actual poaching continues as well. Tanzania's big four—elephants, rhinos, hippopotamus, buffaloes—are threatened, as well as cats of every kind, kudus and gazelles, crocodiles, and many other species.

But these guys—our visitors tonight—are pretty safe. Poachers avoid the giraffe—nothing to gain, little to sell.

I exhale, my brain finally realizing I need oxygen. But neither of us moves nor speaks until the creatures fade back into silent darkness. Even then we only whisper, wondering where they're going and whether they know humans are tucked somnolently inside each of the tents as they chuff through camp. Are they as conscious of us as we are of them?

We bring it up with Nelson, our guide, the next day. "They recognize humans," he says, "but only when they're out in the open, standing on two feet. Humans in tents are just tents, and humans in safari Jeeps are just Jeeps. So they're not afraid. If they saw you encroaching on their territory on foot, you would be an enemy."

Nelson went on to tell us more. "The giraffe—*twiga*—is a fickle creature!" he explains. "They travel in groups for safety, but their social attachments are fluid and quickly changed." He reads to us from his manual that researchers define their groups as "individuals within a square mile moving in the same direction." That's pretty loose! "They don't have vocal chords, so we humans think they're silent," while in truth, their communications might simply be beyond us. Nelson says he's heard them hiss and make a sort of grunt. Sometimes, he says, they whistle at each other, a noise that sounds like a flute. And then for long-distance communication, they use infrasound, which is too low for humans.

A mama twiga and her baby cross languidly in front of our stopped vehicle. We crane our heads and aim our cameras. She looks lazily toward us, nods, and continues on, her tiny charge scampering between her legs to keep up. They're so beautiful and unexpectedly graceful, given their ungainly proportions. Nelson tells us their scientific name—*giraffe camelopardalis*—"camel" plus "leopard." We see its aptness.

"They fight with their necks," continues Nelson. "It's called necking." Huh. "They're quite polygamous." Nelson picks up his manual, thumbs through to the desired page, and begins to read. "In fact, male giraffes are 'sexually nondiscriminating.'" He looks up with an embarrassed half smile, and we sense his discomfort with the topic. Nevertheless, he plows bravely ahead, knowing we Americans are interested in this sort of thing. "'They frequently mount each other, and their same-sex activity is as high as 70 percent.'" He slams the book shut and returns to more comfortable subjects. "Vegetarians, mostly, and acacia trees are their favorite!" We ask about the calf we saw. "Foal," he corrects. He tells us that giraffe pregnancies last up to 460 days (15-plus months!) and that they give birth standing up. "The foal comes out head-and-front-legs-first, drops to the ground, and is lucky if it doesn't break its neck!"

Mwagusi Safari Camp is one of several lodgings in Ruaha National Park, and it's generally where Bega Kwa Bega sends its partners. It is luxury. Mwagusi is a place where the visitor is treated to the poshest in food and lodgings, where one is cosseted and cared for in extravagance, where one can enjoy either formal discourse or impromptu lectures, delivered by expertly trained naturalists. There is entertainment and conversation and relaxation. One day I asked my first-year students if anyone had been to Mwagusi. Not a single hand went up. The same question posed to my second-year class produced two responses. One man had driven bus for a local tour company; a second had worked in groundskeeping at the camp. Few Tanzanians can afford to go on safari, but the parks add significantly to the national revenue. BKB's philosophy is that when you visit Tanzania, you need to see as much as possible; you need to understand the country to understand your partner congregation and its community. At your congregation, you'll undoubtedly meet some of the nation's rural poor. The medium-sized city of Iringa will provide you with a window into the middle and business classes. Dar es Salaam, like most big cities, shows you a mix of everything—the wealthiest, the poorest, and the whole lot between. But perhaps few things can teach so much about what shapes the underlying culture of the country than a safari expedition. It's a lesson in topography and wildlife, both flora and fauna. It's a lesson about national appreciation. You see first-hand Tanzania's heart for preservation of its natural wealth and way of life. You see conservation efforts on display, enjoy Tanzanian hospitality to the extreme, and witness their absolute joy in who they are.

Cultural and conservation talk aside, when all is said and done, when I think of safari, I am transported back to the night of the giraffes. It is as vivid a memory as any. And I have many. I have been to Ruaha now several times.

Lions eating a kill: Our safari vehicle sits so close that we can hear bones crunching and saliva dripping. The pride has taken down a water buffalo. The big old male *simba* has had his fill of the choicest parts, and now he lolls in the sun on a nearby stone. Harem and cubs are deep into ribs, legs, and head. None of them pay us any attention, so our driver circles around and inches us closer. We hear flies swarming for their share.

Hippos snorting: I sit alone on an April night in the darkness of a Ruaha Riverlodge guest cabin. The Great Ruaha River below me teems with "river horses"—*kiboko*. The camp brochure says the snorting is a sexual come-on in mating season. Our safari guide says, "They're farting." I have a hard time feeling much fondness for hippos. They spend about sixteen hours a day in the water, coming out at night to do a bit of hunting or exploring. When they yawn at each other, it's not because of fatigue; it's because they're threatening each other. They're fiercely territorial, and like many creatures, they mark territory by defecating. But they've developed it into an athletic art form: they spin their tails mid-act to whirl the shit everywhere. Ugh. At the very least, they should be quiet about it.

Elephants—*tembo*—with ears a-flap: Those ears are amazing. They use them for cooling, but they're also sensory, so with ears a-flap, they hear better. They use them as a threat as well. Mama elephant comes at our safari vehicle with her ears a-flap, the engine roars to life, and we take off at full speed. In our rear view, I watch the "aunties" surrounding the adorable little calf that drew us too near.

Once on an earlier safari, walking back from the dining hall, I rounded the curve toward my banda and found a huge male elephant blocking its entrance. Constantine was around forty years old, and he loved to mingle with human society. He was the camp owner's best buddy, and he probably wouldn't have attacked anyone, but I didn't know that the first time I met him. My fellow-traveler friend Elinor and I were going to our tents for siesta. Six-year-old

Wema, our friend Joe Lugalla's daughter, was between us. We turned the corner, and there was Constantine a yard or so in front of us... ears a-flap. My first thought was "where's my camera?" He took a step toward us and held out his trunk. My second thought—and Elinor's—was "grab the kid and run!" In fact, the second hadn't even materialized in our brains before maternal instinct kicked in. Wema's feet never touched the ground. That evening, Joe and Wema called Wema's mother back home in New Hampshire to tell her that Elinor and I had saved her life!

That local story about the elephant who wandered into Iringa and fell into one of those six-foot concrete gullies designed for channeling rain was something I heard from so many different sources that I suspect it's true. It wasn't hurt, but it had to remain there several days, bellowing pitifully, until a mechanical crane could be brought in to lift it out. That tembo might well have been Constantine. Rumor had it he was sometimes sighted on the edges of the city. Iringans were fond of Constantine stories, because by all reports, Constantine was curious about human companionship. He'd initiated numerous human encounters, never with aggression or mischievous intent. I wonder about Constantine. Perhaps the *Loxodonta* company around Ruaha didn't satisfy him.

The last time I saw Constantine was at the outskirts of Ruaha Park as our bus trundled over the boundary. I know it was him because Peter, who was at the wheel again—and who was a former safari park guide—told me so, pointing out his lack of a tusk (one lost in a fight as a younger fellow) and the distinctive ragged edges around his ears, acquired in longevity. It was with great sadness a year later that Peter told me Constantine had been found dead, the victim of poachers. He'd been shot, his huge body left to lie where it fell, his one remaining tusk ruthlessly hacked away.

Impalas, water buffaloes, hyraxes, lions, leopards, zebras, monkeys and baboons, ostriches, crocodiles...

As I write, I try in vain throughout the above to use "who" for the creatures in my discussion, and my grammar program keeps flagging and changing it to "that." The lesson, I suppose, is that I shouldn't anthropomorphize. However, there should be an obvious way to honor them with more intelligence than inanimate objects. They're each equally as intelligent as we humans are. The fact that they don't possess *human* intelligence doesn't mean they're not smart. They have intelligence peculiar to their species. To compare their understanding with ours is really apples and oranges. I don't have elephant intelligence or giraffe acumen or lion intellect or—obviously—hippo aptitude.

Clearly, safari doesn't happen every day. This particular semester, for instance, I visited Ruaha's National Park only twice. Over a long weekend when Tumaini cancelled Thursday and Friday classes to honor a state holiday, Russ and I stayed in neighboring cabins at Ruaha's Riverlodge. That's when I heard cavorting hippos. Later, when Kurt joined me for two weeks, bringing a group of eleven other visitors from New Hampshire, we enjoyed Mwagusi. Safari is wonderful, but one doesn't need a special outing to appreciate wildlife in Tanzania. Domestic life, even in cities, is framed by animals.

Wild dogs—*mbwa*—and chickens—*kuku*—are the musical backdrop here to all my daydreams. I hear soft chicken cluckings beneath everything, whether I'm walking to town center, hiking back up the hill, negotiating Tumaini campus, driving out in the countryside, or sitting in one of the rural community churches…where chickens are carried up to the altar at church services, wrapped in rags and squawking, and placed in the offering baskets. And on occasion, they're brought to me as gifts.

Many of our neighbors keep hens. I buy their eggs, thirty eggs to a flat, 10,000 T-shillings per flat. I boil them a dozen at a time, and Russ and I have mashed eggs on toast for breakfast—about twenty cents an egg. Eggs are the chief protein in many diets here.

I fall asleep at night listening to wild dogs baying across the valley. If I wake during the night, I hear the owl that lives in the branches over our house. His hooting is as full of longing as the dogs,' or perhaps it's my own human longing I hear. Indeed, many nights, my life feels full of animal wildness. Do I know these creatures? I feel as if I do. We share a kinship in the shadows. The quietest are the nearest and most intimate. When it's still, I catch the tiny, almost imperceptible skitter of geckos in the ceiling or the soft flutter of moths against the screen. But of all the night creatures, the most obvious are those dogs. *Don't Let's Go to the Dogs Tonight,* Alexandra Fuller's account of a white childhood in Africa, is at my bedside. I read it, and Fuller's shimmering phrases play through my mind as I lay awake and drone through my dreams as I sleep.

Dogs live all around the Wilolesi area, kept as security for chickens and other farm animals. Often their baying is near, just outside our gate. Sometimes it rises to hysteria, and then I imagine these canine sentinels warding off something wild. Their more likely target is a drunkard staggering down from the Hilltop, taking a leak against a fence. He should be grateful, I think. Those dogs might well be saving his life, their noisy barking keeping him awake and alert to the car racing past, his drinking buddy at the wheel. I don't know the statistics, but Tanzanians know that nighttime inebriation makes for danger. Printed on every wine box are bold words in all caps—DON'T DRINK AND WALK. YOU WILL DIE. And so the howling dogs might be saving lives. One dog's howl begets another, and soon the chorus rises and falls, rises and falls, then fades away to return in waves throughout the night.

Beyond that first canine ring comes an answering echo, maybe dogs, maybe—I'm learning—baboons. Large communities of olive baboons live in the mountains around Iringa. Perhaps hunting troops of males are out. Baboons—*nyani*—aren't fussy about what they eat. They woo-hoo their presence, confident in the safety of darkness. Occasionally in wee hours, 2:00 or 3:00 a.m., I hear shrill barks and screams, eerie and otherworldly, certainly not human, probably baboon. They sound intentional. Does a baboon know his own weirdness?

In the daylight hours, the animal presence is more domestic. Neighborhood roosters wake me every morning. By eight, Russ and I head to campus for the day. We bump down the hill, and silent milk cows—*ng'ombe*—gaze at us through rough board fences, their cuds dripping with grassy saliva. One Saturday morning, on foot instead of driving the van, we pass the house where another Tumaini professor lives. His eight-year-old daughter, Elizabeta, is milking their cow, and we stop to watch. It's a lovely small brown creature with black doe-eyes, the rope around her neck tied to a stake. Elizabeta plops herself down on her milking stool and scoots under the cow's flank, grabs a teat, and pulls the milk into her bucket. I know how that feels; I know the flank where Elizabeta rests her forehead is warm and smooth, and that she feels the firm strength of bone resting just under skin, that when she pulls her head away, for just a moment, she feels the roughness of the fur as she rubs against its grain. My teenage years were spent on my stepfather's dairy farm where I often helped with the nightly milking. Everything was mechanized, but he taught me how to milk a cow by hand because it was important to "know how a cow feels." At eight, Elizabeta is more proficient than I ever was. In no time, her bucket sloshes with warm white; she grins at us, waves, and heads toward the house where her mother waits.

Most mornings, we dodge goats—*mbuzi*—as soon as we turn onto the university access road. Sometimes we wait while an entire herd crosses, a small boy urging them with his stick, grinning and waving at us in apology, tacitly acknowledging that he can do little to control his charges. I wonder each day where they're going. There are no pastures here; only city. I suppose that the goats spend the day following ditches where weeds grow and drifting from low-hanging tree branch to scruffy bush. The child in charge trails behind with his stick. When a goat doesn't immediately do what he wants, he gives it a smart crack. And when the stick fails, he administers a hard kick. Students kicked the lone goat that wandered into Academic Hall mid-lecture too. He amused me; I would have let him stay, but the students treated him as a nuisance. Africans tend to define animal "rights" differently than we Americans—no SPCA or PETA in a country where human hunger traditionally trumps a beast's existence. There's little luxury for pets.

Although there's a cat—*paca*—at the Hilltop who's regarded fondly. He's a working cat, and he has the run of the compound, and often ours as well, where he'll sneak inside if the back door is left open. If he has a name, I've not learned it. He's scrawny, doubtfully from a lack of prey or restaurant scraps, more likely from worms.

A compound owned by a wealthy man on the opposite side of town boasts a couple of peacocks. When I visited Iringa the first time, a lone camel grazed along Uhuru Road near the vacant airfield, but that camel has disappeared. Neither peacocks nor camels are indigenous. One elegant creature is, however. The agama or Kenyan rock lizard is by far the most stylish beast in all of Tanzania, and one of him lives among the rocks in our wall. *Mjusi* is shy. My first sighting is a flash of turquoise, as blue and intense as Zanzibar's coast. The next time, weeks later, after the rainy season ends, I catch him sun bathing along a ledge. Wary but stretched to his full eighteen-inch length, his long blue iridescence contrasted by a chic red head. He locks eyes with me for a second before glinting back into the wall. What style! What panache! What a difference from his little bug-eyed gecko cousins inside.

At Holy Trinity, our church in New Hampshire, we buy chickens, ducks, or goats as alternative gifts at Christmastime. Recipients get a card with a photo; the people of Isimani get the animals themselves. Each of my grandchildren has received either a dozen chickens or a dozen ducks for their Christmas stockings. The picture on the gift card is really cute, but I'm guessing none of them truly appreciate the contribution yet or even think of it as a gift at all. "Oh yeah… again with the ducks." It's just something Grandma does.

Cute ducks are a different story in Isimani. Once a busload of Holy Trinity folks were returning to Iringa after a long Sunday visit. It was loud. On the one hand, we were exhausted, emotionally spent, because one can balance on a pedestal under alleluias of gratitude just so long before breaking down. On the other, because we didn't know what to do with all our emotion, we were talking, talking, talking, trying to process what we'd seen. We were accompanied by the bus's bumps and crunches on a lonely, rutted stretch of dirt.

Ahead we spotted a single kanga-clad figure flagging us down. She had something bunched up in her dress folds. Joe motioned for our driver to pull over and open the door. Some quick Swahili was exchanged and the bundle was torpedoed in, squawking and flailing. The woman shouted *"Asante sana! Asante sana!"* and waved us off, both hands over her head. We heard her ululating as we drove away. Our Holy Trinity donations had provided a year of school tuition for her son. She had no money to give us, so she gave us her only duck.

One of the first days after moving in at Wilolesi, I go to the kitchen to begin supper preparations. Our kitchen is "fully stocked" with utensils (two aluminum sauce pans, two plastic dinner plates, two soup spoons, one dinner fork, assorted cups and drinking glasses, and a dull paring knife) and linens (a cotton dish towel hanging on the wall near the sink). I reach out to grab the towel, and as I move it, something small and dark skitters from underneath it and disappears behind the sink. It might be a mouse, something I've never feared, but the surprise catches me off guard. I yelp, and Russ comes running. He laughs, promises to protect me, and assures me he'll take care of the situation if it reappears. It doesn't.

The second time I feel fearful over critters is almost too silly and embarrassing to report. It happens because one evening when I come to bed, I notice a flock (gaggle? crowd? pod?) of baby lizards clinging to the wall beside my bed. For several moments, I watch in fascination tinged with horror. I notice most of all—and with sudden tenderness, in spite of myself—their little balloon feet, and that small detail is the only thing that keeps me from squashing them. I am aware that to make a move toward them of any sort will send them scurrying into hiding, into cracks in the wall or above and into the ceiling, which is exactly what happens when they finally sense my presence. One lone baby stays glued to the wall, whether frightened into a frozen state or just defiant. Whatever the reason, I admire his tenacity. I leave him. Once ensconced in bed under the mosquito netting, I take occasional glances his way; he remains until I finally fall asleep. In the morning, he's gone.

Lizards are useful, and though I might have originally felt squeamish about them, their presence is soon a comfort, especially when I remember all the smaller species each one eliminates—flies, mosquitoes, and especially spiders.

Spiders: I encountered my first really, really big one the first week in Iringa. I called Russ to deal with it. A month or so into my tenure, I become brave. Sitting in the middle of our dining room floor one day is a really, really big gray-with-white-spots number. She's just sitting there. We stare eye-to-eye for a few seconds, considering how to deal with each other. Russ is not around; it's just the two of us. I'm a grown woman, but she's huge! Easily six inches leg-to-leg, her body alone is about three inches across. I back up and inch myself down the hallway to the storage closet and find a spray can of poison. Holding it out in front of me like a gun, I approach her step by slow step. She doesn't move. "I'm not afraid to use this," I say. "Back off and leave me alone." She sits. I spray. She sits. I spray again, more heavily. She rears up and looks as if she's going to attack. I scoot back, run down the hall, and shut myself behind my steel bedroom door. By the time I venture out to check on her, she's gone, and I never see her again. I choose to believe that the poison had little to no effect, that she crawled back under the floorboards or behind the ceiling tiles, and that she's gone back to sharing mosquitoes with the geckos.

On Uhuru Road, just north of Iringatown center, Monday through Friday at eight thirty in the morning, a pair of donkeys—*punda*—pull a small wooden cart loaded with lumber. Hardly bigger than a wheelbarrow, the little wagon could have been managed by a man alone were it not weighed down with freight. A guy in ragged work clothes walks alongside, stick in hand, and a third donkey trots closely behind. Five days a week on our drive to Tumaini, we pull up behind them, slowing the van to a crawl until traffic clears enough to maneuver out and around. The two creatures pulling the dray are sway-backed and look both fatigued and aggrieved. They plod. Each step is an effort. Normally donkeys have sweet faces with huge dark eyes. The fearful, imploring eyes on these fellows bespeak sadness. My guess is it has something to do with that stick. Still, they hold their heads high, ridiculously large ears pointing skyward. The effect is that the ears are the only things keeping them standing.

This goes on for four months. Then one morning the dray is gone, and one of the donkeys lies in the packed dirt at the side of the road. As we pass by, I can see him trying to raise his head. His tail twitches, but that's all.

The second day, he's in the same condition. By the third day, he's dead.

At that time, a professor emeritus from the university dies. This man was beloved and revered by many, and he's being given a funeral with full honors as a very important person. On Friday, classes are cancelled so students and faculty can go to his home to show respect to the family. On Saturday, his body lies in state for viewing. His funeral and internment the following day are presided over by the bishop of the Iringa diocese. Several thousand mourners are in attendance. Dignitaries come from all over the country, some even from Dar es Salaam. I hadn't personally known the man, but his son, a current professor at the university, is a good friend of mine, so I participate in everything as completely as I can. All the while, Hellen is at my side, protecting me from committing offensive cultural mistakes. She dresses me in the appropriate traditional clothes, leads me through receiving lines at the proper times and at the proper pace, all the time whispering in my ear. Thanks to Hellen, I think I say the right words and bow at all the right moments.

I never weep for this man. I cry instead for the donkey. I cry at the roadside; I cry again alone at night. For me that little animal is a symbol of all the small creatures, human and animal alike, who spend their lives in toil, often under difficult circumstances, suffering pain and derision, and finally dying alone without recognition. No one pays attention as the little guy lies at the side of the road. No one checks to see if he's in pain. No one notices his last breath. No one even comes to remove his body until several days later when it turns offensive.

The title of this chapter includes the word "friend." When I think of my time here, of the friendships I've made, friendships with nonhumans are as strong as those with humans. The animals I met and/or lived with accepted me no more and no less than they would have accepted this country's natural-born human residents. Animals never cared, never even noticed the color of my skin, the fact that I spoke no Swahili, or that oftentimes my behaviors tended toward foolish cultural gaffes. When they laughed behind my back, the laughter was no different for me than for native Tanzanians. No animal ever called me Mzungu.

Animals never judged the whys of my intentions toward them. At the same time, they taught me how to care for and respect the little guy; how to unconditionally give, even when I don't expect a reward; how to be who I'm supposed to be, honoring my own particular gifts and talents. The other half of that coin is not to try to be someone I'm not supposed to be. No animal I ever met attempts to be something other than what she is. Agama is agama; gecko is gecko. Dog, elephant, giraffe, donkey (yes, even hippo), they're all 100 percent focused on being who they're designed to be. My animal friends teach me a lot.

14

The Girl in the Restaurant

It felt as if we left Iringa in a hurry. Although we'd published the dates multiple times, everyone seemed surprised we were leaving. "It is impossible," announced the woman in the registrar's office when I asked for the forms to report final grades. "You must remain until at least the middle of July, when final exams are scheduled for the sections you teach." Neither Russ nor I had ever seen a schedule for final exams (because it had never been published, indeed had not until now been decided upon), and when we'd bought airline tickets, we'd assumed it would be reasonable to fly out a week after the semester—excuse me, *term*—ended. So ten days before the end, I found myself in the administration office yet again, pleading for rescheduling. Twenty-four hours later, 250 shell-shocked students who'd thought they had another two weeks to cram dutifully filed into the Science Center lecture hall. I handed out the exam, answered preliminary questions, and left them in the hands of their university-appointed proctors.

A flurry of activity followed. The next day, Law faculty suddenly announced a farewell dinner for Russ and me that very night at one of Iringa's best restaurants. I took out the little black dress and heels I'd yet had an occasion to wear; Russ donned suit and tie. In typical Tanzanian fashion, instead of toasts or farewell speeches, the professors asked each of us to innumerate all the ways we thought Tumaini should improve itself. "We would like some day to equal the practices and excellences of an American institution."

Apparently, the evening signaled the reality of our going; the next day, the gifts began. As we climbed into our van after classes, Atu from administration asked for a ride to the marketplace to "pick up an errand," and the errand turned out to be a new dress for me from her local seamstress. Another full outfit—skirt, blouse, and matching headwrap—arrived from Beata and her friends. Edgar brought me a set of straw serving trays with my name woven in: "Dr. Doroth." Ironically, the afternoon he delivered them at our office, the Mbuli boys arrived at precisely the same moment to complain about their last grades. Michael Emmanuel announced quite firmly, "Madam, we did not contribute willingly to this gift." There were more: Iringa baskets and batiks, tinga-tingas and beaded bracelets, handwritten letters, a carved wooden nativity set and other statues, a beaded Maasai headpiece. Each day that week, we left our office with our hands full.

And there were the opposite, appeals. Students asked for letters, recommendations for graduate study and jobs, letters of referral or transfer to other schools, formal requests for tuition waivers and extensions. Some wanted advice on applying for study in the US; one asked for actual sponsorship. We did the best we could. But when Beata returned to make one last attempt for a monetary contribution, I turned her down flat. "You will still write to me and be my American professor friend, yes?" Yes.

Not just students. A faculty member wanted written advice for his newly-formed committee. The dean of Student Affairs handed me five professional journal articles to edit. Russ was asked to speak at one last Student Law Association event. I think we were gratified to know we'd been appreciated, but we felt pressured, actually downright harried. It was difficult to remain calm, let alone cheerful. The strangest came from the Indian professor who brought his eighteen-year-old son and asked Russ to hire him and take him back to the US. That one got denied on the spot.

When I think of those final days, I think mostly of the towering pile of research papers—a five-pager for each of the 200-odd students in my combined classes—that I managed to grade and return within seven days. It was impressive. Russ helped me wrangle their bulk into the van and back to Wilolesi where we heaped them up and took a photo for posterity (mine). I knew that once back in the States, I'd think twice before complaining about a workload.

Finally, there was the job of leaving Wilolesi, and it was difficult, so much more difficult than I'd expected, not for the physical labor as much as the emotional. I went around snapping photos. My bedroom: crooked blinds hanging from mismatched window frames; the mattress too short for the bedstead; dusty, ragged straw carpet; the wooden wardrobe with its locking drawers (no keys). Our living spaces: sofa and chairs graced with pillows I'd covered, grouped around the fireplace we never lit; our Western-style kitchen (still no electric lighting); the third bedroom we used for hanging wet laundry. Outside, I snapped both the front porch, where we sometimes sat in the afternoon sun, and the glorious view over the valley it afforded. I walked out the gate and over the upper lane toward the school and soccer fields, past the NGO complexes whose iron fences were hung with bougainvillea. I stopped to sit for a moment on the low branch of a tree where the road forked. I breathed in and tried to memorize odors: dry dust, African spice, city livestock, sweet hibiscus and musky acacia leaf. My camera wouldn't catch everything.

I once asked BKB's Pastor Julie what she missed most when she left Iringa for her home in Minnesota. "The dirt walkway along Uhuru Drive," she said. "The stretch between the big tree on the corner and Hasty Tasty's front porch, where it gets wide and dusty. I see the street vendors spreading out their wares, hear the work-hard bird calling, smell spices from the market, and feel leaves from the bushes brushing my arms. When I start walking that path in daydreams, I know it's time to come back." Thinking of her words now, I turn my camera toward the ground to catch the ruts in the road.

The morning we left Wilolesi for Dar, our old friend Dani arrived with the Tumaini Land Rover at seven. I smiled, remembering the morning six months earlier when I'd waited to be picked up at that exact hour, how the Swahili-speaking driver wouldn't have arrived until one in the afternoon, and how Lotte had had to rescue me. This morning, Dani was accompanied by that exact same driver.

He helped carry out our things, locked up the house, collected our keys, and drove off toward Tumaini with our borrowed van.

Cosmos stood near the gate at attention. He and Russ shook hands, and Russ thanked him profusely for taking such good care of us. It was my turn. Cosmos saluted me. I stretched out a hand, changed my mind, and reached my arms up around his neck. We hugged for a long moment, neither saying anything. Then I heard a gravelly whisper, "Goodbye, Professor Mama." Russ, Dani, and I climbed aboard the Rover, drove through the gate one last time, and headed toward the highway. The last sound from Wilolesi was the clank of the gate behind us. That was the last glimpse of my "little brother."

Fast-forward three years. Back home in New Hampshire, I sent a money order via Western Union to a former Tumaini student of mine. Zeph and I had, over months of electronic communication, become close friends. But back at Tumaini itself, he hadn't singled himself out, hadn't drawn attention, and I have to admit—with a bit of awkwardness on my part—I'd ignored him. He was one of those quiet, hardworking students who pass their assignments in on time, earn good grades, and never ask for special favors. As I remembered it, our relationship had been cordial but distant enough so that I had a hard time even remembering his name. He took care of that in his first e-mail a couple of weeks after I left Tanzania: "Hello Professor, it's me Zeph, the one you always call Said." Like I said, awkward. I had indeed always called him "Said." He'd approach me after class to ask a question, and I'd routinely mistake him for another student. Zeph was dark and fine-boned with a mustache, which he couldn't ever quite eliminate. Said wore white Muslim robes and a white fez. I clearly should have recognized the difference between the two, but I couldn't ever quite get them straight. By all rights, Zeph should have been perturbed by this, but he wasn't.

After his first tentative e-mail, Zeph began enthusiastically telling me about his home (near Kilimanjaro), his family (a mother, a grandmother, and some younger siblings) and his future plans) to use his law degree to work for equal rights for women. He wrote about his activities, about how he'd gone to his district commissioner to plead for the beginnings of a town library so that his sisters could have books and about how he'd worked at odd jobs during all his school vacations to help keep the younger kids in school. He wrote weekly, sometimes even daily, whenever he had computer access.

A year into our electronic friendship, Zeph asked for permission to call me "Bibi" [Grandmother]. I knew that to be a huge compliment. I gave permission, and once given, my role immediately changed from interested former professor to trusted advisor. Then in his final year at Tumaini, he asked for my opinion on course selection, then on a choice of topic for final thesis, and on to advice about pursuing a career. The sticking point was always money. With no father or grandfather in the picture, Zeph was responsible for a lot of people. At the culmination of his college years, he sent me a picture of himself, a rather formal portrait in graduation robes, smiling as he held up a diploma. In it, he looks much older than his years.

After graduation, he moved to Dar to try to make enough money to pay the fees for the extra year of classes the government requires before one is allowed to practice law. The classes don't amount for much; they're mostly a way for Tanzania to collect revenue, but no one gets exempted. Without the extra year, Zeph's career was dead in the water.

Another full year went by. Still, Zeph was unable to come up with the money, and now—finally—he sent his first (and only) plea: "Please, Bibi, I need sponsorship." Again, I emphasize that this was his first request, even in the midst of a student culture that encourages begging from foreigners. Zeph had remained above the fray. Then and now, every aspiration began with "God willing" and every hope ended with "God provides." To date, it had felt that God hadn't. And so I finally made the decision to send him money.

I withdrew $200 cash to take to the Western Union office, filled out the papers, and handed over the money. The forms required a question/answer for the recipient so as to prove his legitimacy. I filled in the blanks with "How to use?" and "Law school," and then I went home and e-mailed Zeph.

Three days later, I sat wondering if the entire relationship had been a scam. Then I felt guilty for entertaining the idea. We had an honest relationship. He was respectful. He was conniving. He was sincere. He was a crook. I ate, drank, slept, talked, breathed, and ambled in ambivalence. Finally, it occurred to me that if Zeph had indeed scammed me, it was a damn good scam: three solid years of effort and setup. He deserved the money as a gift without the law school string attachment. Really, if he now wasted the money on some fly-by-night financial scheme or bought himself fancy electronic equipment or spent it on alcohol and drugs, I had the eternal satisfaction of knowing it was hard-earned.

But I couldn't really believe he'd scammed me. Maybe someone had intercepted the money. Those pirates from Nairobi that everyone fears...

Maybe he was mugged and robbed as he left the Western Union office.

Maybe he'd been left for dead in a back alley of Dar es Salaam and neither his family nor I would ever know what happened.

I waited.

And I knew I'd done the right thing. Sending Zeph the money was on my part a conviction of the soul. Conviction is not wasted. No act of mercy or charity or love is ever wasted. In the total scheme of the universe—in God's kingdom—an act done for good is *good*.

Two more days passed. I tracked my money online and learned that someone had picked it up in Dar. Was it Zeph? I e-mailed him to ask but no reply. Perhaps I would never hear from him again. Or—more likely—because Zeph worked long hours, piecemeal, and because he didn't own a computer, he simply hadn't had the chance to get himself to an Internet café.

When I knew Zeph as a student, I hadn't paid him much attention. With so many students jockeying for a claim on my time, I hadn't pursued friendship. He'd waited in the background, gently correcting me each time I called him by the wrong name, patient to wait until I could afford him attention. He'd waited through that whole semester, and even on my return to the States, he'd waited through months of e-mails, patient to take incremental steps in developing a relationship, securing my trust.

On day six, I opened my laptop to read, "Hellow dearest Bibi, God has given you to me but I do not deserve. My thankfulness to you for your faith. Even faith in me. I promise I will make you proud of me. Your always loving Tanzanian Grandson, Zeph. PS God Provides."

Zeph *has* made me proud. I am honored to call him my grandson. Each time I've returned to Tanzania, we've connected to share a meal, to chat, to hug. He has a great job working for an international firm that connects artists and artisans with sponsorship, but the road hasn't been easy. Soon after renting his first apartment in Dar, the family sent his younger brother to him to shepherd through secondary school. Zeph's entry-level banking job provided just enough funds to cover living expenses and school fees. It was a good job but one that included risk as he was tasked with carrying funds back and forth after hours. One night as he climbed into a taxi for the trip across town, he felt a blow to the head. The last thing he remembered was someone smashing a rag into his face, over his nose and mouth. The following morning, the police found him sprawled across an alleyway and barely alive. He doesn't remember the ambulance ride nor the surgery to put his leg back together nor the shunt in his chest to drain fluid nor his first days in the hospital while the drugs cleared his system. Both the money and the bank computer entrusted to him were gone. To add to the injury, the bank insisted Zeph's carelessness caused the "accident." They refused to pay medical expenses, then billed him for the lost computer. Zeph and brother moved in with friends, but as soon as he was fit, he got himself another job. Schooling had to be suspended for a term, but today, the brother is a proud secondary graduate and pursuing a college degree.

Most mornings here in the States, I go online to read the *Tanzanian Daily News*. As in the US, the lead story is almost always something horrific. A lorry, loaded with furniture and a dozen passengers catching a ride, careens out of control and goes off the road, over the edge. There are no survivors. An outbreak of cholera in western regions has caught the attention of the World Health Organization. In the north, three albinos' bodies are found, mutilated and decapitated for sale in witchcraft; the district commissioner is introducing more legislation to stop the practice. The gruesome almost seems routine, until one morning I read this: "To date this year in Dar es Salaam, three dozen people have died in assault-and-robbery schemes by criminals posing as taxi drivers. Their modus operandi includes drugging, beating, and leaving the victim for dead." Again, I hear Zeph: "God provides."

Gugami e-mailed me today. I am so happy to hear from him. I don't remember him. He remembers me (one of me; two hundred of them). It would be wonderful if all of them were e-mailing. I couldn't ever keep up, of course. I couldn't keep up with them when I lived there, when they were right in front of me, when I saw them every day; so how could I keep up now? Gugami is a symbol to me of all of them. A reminder. Each is precious. Each has a voice, and it's interesting that that voice is louder and clearer now than it ever was when they were right in front of me. Students in Tanzania are not necessarily used to having their opinions heard. Now in e-mail Gugami has begun to have all sorts of opinions…and plans and dreams. He describes his thesis to me, tells me his parents are both dead and that he's being supported by his aunt and uncle, and identifies his substitute parents as "peasants."

Everyone is a peasant. A Minnesota pastor tells a joke about visiting a rural congregation near Iringa. He asked a parishioner what his job was, and the man answered, "I'm a piss-ant." Confused, the pastor went to a second man and asked the same question. "I'm a piss-ant." The third: "I'm a piss-ant." I chuckle now as I read Gugami's e-mail, thankful his spelling clarifies the status.

Gugami makes me long for so many others. I'm fairly confident I'll see some of them when I return; students, for instance, who find jobs or family in Iringa; people who teach or work at Tumaini. Zeph: I'll meet him for supper in Dar es Salaam one day. Falres: he'll spend a year in the US teaching and studying. Atu: she'll send me a gift—a wooden carving of Jesus the Shepherd—hand carried by Falres. Shafeen at Hasty Tasty, Elia in Maasai Matebete, Mbata from the marketplace, Robert the Hilltop waiter, Tuti at the Lutheran Center, Grace and Peter and Dennis and Wingred. Hellen, who I'll meet for dinner with her new husband when I return. The list is long.

Longer still is the list of those folks I doubt I'll see, even though every one of them was influential in shaping my stay. Paramount is Cosmos. It would be impossible for me to find his home again. I don't even know his last name.

Once when I was in D.C. visiting with my daughter, we went to Denny's for breakfast after church on a Sunday morning. There were six of us—Kurt, our daughter, son-in-law, two grandkids, and I. As we were shown to our booth—chatting, jostling, generally kidding around with the children—I thought I saw someone I recognized. In other words, I have a vague memory of seeing someone whom I thought looked familiar; but on the other hand, maybe I made that up. I ignored my hunch and went back to playing with my family.

I *know* I didn't make this up: as we left the restaurant, I *saw* Salha Ramadhani. And I know this: failing to recognize and acknowledge her is one of my greatest disappointments.

Salha was my first-year law student at Tumaini. She was a good student, interested and interesting. Salha is Indian, and in Iringa—in Tanzania—Indians are business people. I was told that their success was sometimes resented, that some feared they took too many opportunities. In downtown Iringa, the largest and most complete hardware store was Indian-owned, as was the bicycle shop, an appliance store, a car dealership, a fabric store, and the mattress shop. Indians ran one of the best restaurants. They were a strong presence. But they were treated with a bit of distrust. It was the closest thing to racism that I saw.

In the apartment complex, for instance, the Indians—who lived crowded together, all in one block; who cooked together, watched each other's children, and socialized apart from everyone else—were often disparaged. I heard folks complain that the children were "poorly behaved" and "poorly disciplined." They were clean; it was allowed; and they kept their yard neat, but their cooking smelled.

I could only surmise that Salha got at least some of that treatment. I knew nothing about her family situation, whether she lived on campus or off, whether she was a scholarship student or paid tuition. The sum total of my Salha knowledge came from the classroom where she was always ready with an answer, wrote with both flair and correctness, and was disposed to smile. At the end of class sessions when other students swarmed me with entreaties and elbowed each other with impatience, Salha held back and waited politely.

Seeing her in Washington happened like this. As we gathered ourselves to leave the restaurant, someone held the door for us and smiled at me. It was a grin that involved her whole face, and there was recognition in her eyes. I had that quick notion of something familiar you sometimes get in a dream, but in that instant, with my family urging me on toward the door, I chose to remind myself that knowing someone who worked in a Washington restaurant was impossible. And so I let my granddaughter pull me along into the parking lot. We stopped a moment on the pavement; did someone drop something? Or did a kid tell a joke we had to laugh at? And in my peripheral vision, I saw Salha come toward me. She recognized me, but so far, only my subconscious saw her. The family carried me toward the car. We climbed in and buckled up, and then we drove away.

The following day, I headed back home to New Hampshire. Over the next week, Salha bubbled up from my subconscious and made herself known. I argued and doubted, but the idea wouldn't go away. I told myself not to be silly. What would Salha be doing in D.C.? On the third day, I told my husband about my suspicions, laughing at myself, making a joke. He didn't laugh. In fact he encouraged me to do something about it, so I made the phone call and connected with the restaurant manager.

"Do you have a young woman named Salha working at the restaurant? From India?"

"Not understand you. What you want, please?" Whoever was on the other end of the call spoke about as much English as I her first language. Spanish? Furthermore, for reasons of privacy and legality, she probably couldn't easily give out information. I left my name, my phone number, and e-mail address. Then I called my daughter and asked her to stop by to investigate, which she did. She didn't find anyone named Salha. Maybe she didn't work there after all; maybe she was a fellow customer who simply happened to be standing at the door. Maybe it was Salha; maybe not. I guess I'll never know.

Tanzania itself is like Salha. She niggles around the edges of your consciousness, and you have trouble recognizing her. Caught up in your Western priorities and responsibilities, it's not that you're trying to ignore her; you're rather simply too preoccupied to pay attention. Until it's too late.

And so you go back home and do what you can. You read news stories. You write. You try to figure it out. You try to remember. Maybe you make a few phone calls or attempt to connect online. You regret not paying complete attention when you had the chance.

My failure to recognize and connect with Salha when the Universe gave me a chance is precisely and exactly the way I don't want to treat my Tanzanian experience. Lesson learned: don't ignore. And so I answer every e-mail, even when I don't remember the student. I read, even when I don't like what I'm reading or I don't agree with it. You never know when you're going to have the chance to make a relationship, to learn something, to find a friend.

One just shouldn't let anything slip through one's fingers.

When my mind finds itself back in Iringa, it meanders along a dusty mountain path overhung with bougainvillea. It carries on a banter with itinerate street merchants. It munches on samosas at Hasty Tasty under the watchful portrait of Shafeen's beloved spiritual leader. It opens the back door of Wilolesi to Cosmos's knock: "Madam, where are you?" It rests a gaze on sinuous black bodies lounging in the Maasai corner of Uhuru Park, arms and torsos and confident grins inviting me to stare. It waves to the armed guard at the petrol station when we pull our van in for a fillup. It pushes laughingly back at the crowd of students who rush against me after class and carry me all along the hallways to my office, clamoring for my attention every step of the way.

The Iringa of sudden and unbidden moments of memory is cheerful and colorful, redolent of spice and warm with affection. There's rhythm and sound, from the early-morning Mezzuin's first call to worship to the wails of a Pentecostal exorcism to a gentle Swahili rendering of "What a Friend We Have in Jesus." There's the call of the work-hard bird, the quiet cut-cut-a-docket from a chicken coop, and the sonorous night mewling of feral dogs, all mixed with raucous rhythm-and-blues nightlife and angry male voices in a late-night brawl. Iringa is big, loud, pulsating. Iringa in memory defies enumeration and classification. Try as I will, I can't wrap my mind around it, and I can't stop trying.

Again and again, I walk the upper lane in memory, away from Wilolesi toward the school grounds. From this vantage, I see straight across to Gangilonga Rock, Mkwawa's "talking stone." The sun spills its gold onto the mountains. Sunrise or sunset, it's the same. Time doesn't matter. The valley splays out below, to the Clock Tower at Iringa Circle, the Lutheran Cathedral, even Central Market. Wilolesi climbs the Udzungwas west; Gangilonga, east. From my vantage here on the upper lane, I hear wild things, the drone of locusts, the call of a roller bird, the chatter of the rock hyrax. Folks in the middle of the city miss these on a daily basis. I smell jasmine and roses and bougainvillea.

A gate clanks behind me, and giggling girls emerge. It's Catherine and Elizabeta, the two girls from the banana tree house across the way. They've been visiting with the college girls who live at the Canadian NGO behind these walls. Now they surround me and grab my hands, Catherine my right, Elizabeta my left. They grin up at me with their round black faces. "We're so glad we found you," they chime together. "We'll be coming to visit you again if our mother says we may."

For now, I am alone. I have more questions rather than fewer. No real answers. I realize now I'm vulnerable in two cultures, *mzungu* both places, and yet I am always safe.

Glossary

Asante sana. Thank you very much.

Boma. A fort. The Maasai also use this as a term for a building or group house.

Chakula. Food.

Daladala. A small bus.

Duka. A small shop.

Hodi? May I come in?

Kanga. A woman's garment. Traditionally-patterned fabric wrapped and worn as a skirt.

Karibu. Welcome; you're welcome.

Kuku. Chicken.

Malipo. Payment.

Mendazi. A fried pastry, similar to a donut.

Moran. A young man in the Maasai culture; a hunter.

Muezzin adhaan. The Muslim call to prayer.

Mtoto. Baby or small child.

Musungusungu. Going around in circles.

Mzungu A white person; a stranger.

Ndisi. Banana.

Nyani. Baboon.

Nyanya. Tomato.

Punda milia. Zebra.

Pikipiki. Motorcycle.

Pilipili. Peppers.

Pofu. Eland.

Pole. I am sorry.

Polepole. Be careful.

Shuka. The sheet or blanket wrapped for clothing; usually worn by men.

Tango. Cucumber.

Tembo. Elephant.

Twiga. Giraffe.

Ukumbusho. Something to remind us of things past; a souvenir.

Zungu. To go around.

Zuri sana. Very beautiful.

About the Author

Dot Radius Kasik Ph.D. loves to travel and explore different places, peoples, and their cultures. Then she returns home to write about them. What she's discovered through her travels is that much of the learning comes in the writing. She's had the opportunity to teach in several international places, but her favorite is Tanzania where she and her husband return on a yearly basis, teaching at the same Lutheran university she writes about in *Lutheran Mzungu*.

Before Tanzania, Radius-Kasik taught in the English departments at both Salem State in Massachusetts and at the University of New Hampshire. She served as faculty writing consultant at UNH and operates WriteWorthy, a personal academic writing consultancy. She lives with her husband Kurt and their cat Lindy in Portsmouth, New Hampshire.